WHAT P

MW00529847

I heartily recommend *The Lens of Love* by Wei Wei Chang. She is a wonderful person who lives and practices the material in this book. She has been inspirational to many, many people in our congregation and because of the freedom she describes and teaches in this book, many people have been healed and delivered in our church. The news has spread and Wei Wei and her husband, Steve, have helped many people from other churches in the Phoenix area. I don't hesitate to say that as it was for Wei Wei, so it can be for you—life changing!

Thomas Alexander
Senior Pastor, Two Rivers Church, Gilbert, Arizona

Wei Wei's incredible story of working her way through a heartbreaking demotion from an executive position in a major corporation shows how God can take adversity in life and use it to change you for the better. Wei Wei's transparent journey teaches you how to identify and remove tainted lenses of endless striving for significance to enter into God's rest and success. Her story will lead you to a greater clarity of God's unique plan for your life. This book is honest and motivating. It will change your life.

Hal and Cheryl Sacks
Co-founders, BridgeBuilders International Leadership
Network, Phoenix, Arizona
Cheryl Sacks, author of *Prayer Saturated Church;*
Prayer Saturated Family; and Prayer Saturated Kids

Wei and her husband have always been such a precious gift from the Lord to our church family, bringing restoration and breakthrough to many through their inner healing ministry. In her new book, *The Lens of Love*, Wei reveals some of the most intimate and vulnerable places of her heart and story, where you get to witness how God redeems her whole family line from hatred and fear in such a powerful way! In the process, you will receive life-giving keys to reframe your own past and to reconnect with God, your community, and your destiny. I highly recommend *The Lens of Love* to anyone who desires to engage more freely and more fully in God's great end-time work!

Pastor Jason Young
Founding Pastor & Urban Missionary,
Roundtable Church, Hong Kong

I have been friends with Wei Wei and Steve and their family for many years and we have ministered together, doing missions. They bring inner healing and transformation to the world around them. *The Lens of Love* by Wei Wei Chang reveals areas that could be holding us back from thriving in God's purposes or understanding His love and good plans for us. It provides powerful insights and real-life lessons towards a transformation that Wei Wei has personally experienced in her own life. I believe that this book can bless and transform lives on a greater scale!

Jeff Yuen
Founder and Senior Pastor, Soakability Church, Singapore
Author of *Presence-Driven Donkeys:
Bringing Christ to the Streets*

Information without application is just information, but information plus application leads to transformation. The information we have gathered from *The Lens of Love* has deeply filled us. The application of the lessons learned by the Spirit of God within this book has opened our eyes to gloriously transfigure the world around us. The ministry that I serve has grown supernaturally over the past ten years and has remained healthy, largely in part to the ministry we have received from Wei Wei Chang and *The Lens of Love*.

Rev. Matthew H. Geppert
President of South East Asia Prayer Center, Pittsburgh

I am so excited to endorse my dear friend Wei Wei's new book, *The Lens of Love*. In this dynamic story, Wei Wei takes you along on her own journey of leaving behind the lenses of shame and pain that had defined so much of her early life to the point where she began to see who she really is: a daughter who is loved deeply by God. This led her to see others differently as well. Through her life story, she leads us along the path toward freedom and the realization that seeing with new lenses helps to heal the brokenness that has long defined our lives and paints a picture of possibility to see a world captured by the love of Jesus. Read *The Lens of Love* and you'll begin to live loved and to live love.

Rev. Daniel L. Black
Director of Love Fest Global, Hong Kong

THE LENS OF LOVE

A FRESH PERSPECTIVE ON INCREASING INTIMACY WITH GOD, ENHANCING RELATIONSHIPS, AND DISCOVERING CONTENTMENT

THE LENS OF LOVE

A FRESH PERSPECTIVE ON INCREASING INTIMACY WITH GOD, ENHANCING RELATIONSHIPS, AND DISCOVERING CONTENTMENT

WEI WEI CHANG

Published by Author Academy Elite
P.O. Box 43, Powell, OH 43065
www.AuthorAcademyElite.com

Unless otherwise indicated, all Scripture quotations are taken from the Holy Bible, New American Standard Bible, NASB. Copyright © 1960, 1962, 1963, 1968, 1971, 1972, 1973, 1977, 1995 by The Lockman Foundation. Used by permission. www.Lockman.org.

Scripture quotations marked ESV are from The Holy Bible, English Standard Version, copyright © 2001 by Crossway Bibles, a publishing ministry of Good News Publishers. Used by permission. All rights reserved.

Scripture quotations marked NLT are taken from the Holy Bible, New Living Translation, copyright ©1996, 2004, 2015 by Tyndale House Foundation. Used by permission of Tyndale House Publishers, a Division of Tyndale House Ministries, Carol Stream, Illinois 60188. All rights reserved.

Scripture quotations marked AMP are taken from the Amplified Bible, copyright © 1954, 1958, 1962, 1964, 1965, 1987 by The Lockman Foundation. Used by permission.

Scripture quotations marked NKJV are taken from the New King James Version®, copyright © 1982 by Thomas Nelson. Used by permission. All rights reserved.

Scripture quotations marked KJV are from The Authorized (King James) Version. Rights in the Authorized Version in the United Kingdom are vested in the Crown. Reproduced by permission of the Crown's patentee, Cambridge University Press.

Scripture quotations marked NIV are taken from the Holy Bible, New International Version®, NIV®, copyright © 1973, 1978, 1984, 2011 by Biblica, Inc.™ Used by permission of Zondervan. All rights reserved worldwide.

Library of Congress Control Number: 2020918943

Paperback: 978-1-64746-539-1
Hardback: 978-1-64746-540-7
E-book: 978-1-64746-541-4

Available in paperback, hardback, e-book, and audiobook.

Printed in the United States of America

DEDICATION

For my family: Steve, Clarissa, and Noelle:
Your authenticity and desire for truth keep me on my toes
to see things through the lens of love.
I love you so much.

To my parents:
Thank you for passing the legacy of breakthrough,
adventure, service, and diligence to me and
all future generations of our family.

TABLE OF CONTENTS

What People Are Saying i

Dedication xi

Foreword xvii

Acknowledgements xix

A Note to the Reader xxi

PART 1: VISION IMPAIRMENT

Chapter 1: Path of Destruction 3
Failure Is a Blessing in Disguise 3

Chapter 2: Lack of Vision 5
A More Significant Cause of Unhappiness 5

Chapter 3: Original Lens 9
20/20 Vision 9

Chapter 4: Do You Feel Hopeless? 14
Finding Jesus, Finding Hope 14

Chapter 5: Are You Afraid? 19
Jesus, the Light, Dispels the Darkness of Fear 19

Chapter 6: Do You Feel Dissatisfied? 25
Seeing Yourself through Tainted Lenses 25

PART 2: THE DIAGNOSIS

Chapter 7: Visit the Optometrist. 33

   From Physical to Spiritual—Metaphor of a Lens 33

Chapter 8: Tainted Lenses—A Spiritual Perspective 37

   Returning to the Lens of Love 37

Chapter 9: Tainted Lenses—A Historical Perspective 44

   # 1: Family History & Generational Patterns 44

   # 2: Personal Experience 52

Chapter 10: Tainted Lenses—A Soul Perspective. 75

   Revealing Responses. 75

PART 3: VISION CORRECTION

Chapter 11: Repentance 107

   A Divine Exchange. 107

Chapter 12: Forgiveness 110

   The Key to Unlock the Prison Door 110

Chapter 13: The Statue of Abraham Lincoln. 119

   Friendship with God. 119

Chapter 14: God's Word 123

   The Truth Has Set Us Free 123

Chapter 15: Heaven's Vantage Point 125

   Seeing beyond the Natural. 125

Chapter 16: Divine Revelations. 132

   Prophecy and Dreams 132

Chapter 17: God Encounters 137

   Transformation in the Presence 137

PART 4: THROUGH THE LENS OF LOVE

Chapter 18: Miracles. 145
Surrender and Trust 145

Chapter 19: Generational Mandate. 149
Possessing the Land 149

Chapter 20: Significance in Christ. 152
I Am Who He Says I Am. 152

Chapter 21: Intimacy with God 157
Be Thou My Vision. 157

Chapter 22: Journey to the Promised Land 163
Walk with God. 163

Endnotes 167
Tainted Lenses Assessment .173
About the Author. 177

FOREWORD

As the steam-driven, coal-burning locomotive dragged its mile-long string of patched and polished cars along the narrow-gauge track, salty sweat carved narrow trenches down our sooty cheeks. Our band of 15 had entered the far west region of Xinjiang through the high passes of Pakistan. We had encountered the frontier police who'd lightened our load by confiscating our cargo of Christian books and materials, placed us under guard, transported us to Kashgar and then Urumqi. There we were again placed under "protective escort" for our Central China destination of Xian where we would, without ceremony, be deported from the People's Republic.

We had found the Lost Generation, those youth whose parents and grandparents had been "invited to volunteer" to leave their homes and businesses on China's wealthy east coast to come and develop the Great Agricultural Dream of Chairman Mao. Their children and grandchildren were lost in a cross-cultural kaleidoscope so diverse that ancient lenses once clear were now colors of the past.

Chinese Buddhists and Taoists tried to keep their values while the native Uyghurs said their daily prayers to Allah. The children, Chinese and Uyghurs, had a few things in common. They included hard work, difficult study situations, severe climate, broken families, and alcoholism. There were very few smiles. The tension was palatable as we journeyed from rail stop to rail stop, staring through filthy windows as we wondered about and prayed for these young people.

What did they think about? What was their future? How could they come to faith in a God that would never fail them? How would they relate to the outside world if they were fortunate enough to ever escape this trap of the Chairman's folly? These, and many other questions accompanied me during subsequent journeys to China's upper, left- hand corner.

When I began to read *The Lens of Love* by Wei Wei Chang, I was delighted to find one woman's answer to my many questions. Wei's sudden demotion contradicted her Chinese heritage. She saw life through the 6 principles: Honor Your Father, Work Hard, Study Hard, Save Money, Do Not Be Ruled by Your Emotions, Never Show Weakness. Even as a Christian believer, she implemented these values to rapidly ascend in her profession. Having studied her way out of a wilderness to which Mao had sent nonconforming Christian leaders and any others who defied his decrees, she easily climbed the corporate ladder until she attained the rung that would lift her to a corner office.

And then apparent failure brought her to the realization that God has much more for her and for all who will humble themselves before Him. Humility comes through on every page of this book. Finding the end of herself gave Wei Wei the ability to see the love of God which passes human understanding and has released her to minister healing to many others.

A wonderful wife and mother, an accomplished business woman, and now the author of a great book, I trust that all Wei Wei has come through will encourage you to lay down every ambition at the feet of Jesus and allow Him to be your breakthrough.

Mark Geppert
Founder of South East Asia Prayer Center
Author of five books: *The Attack Lambs; Bridges; Stepping Stones; A Faith to Die For;* and *Where Have the Children Gone?*

ACKNOWLEDGEMENTS

I want to thank my husband, Steve, for being my life partner, best friend, and cheerleader. You are God's goodness in my life. Your counsel is full of wisdom and keeps me grounded in truth and love.

Thank you to my daughters:

Clarissa, for helping me with grammar and reading through many chapters of this book. Your feedback and advice reflect wisdom way beyond your age.

Noelle for telling mommy, "It is going to be okay in my difficult times with writing." Your kisses and hugs keep me going.

Thank you, Helen Izek, for being my editor and for taking on the challenge of making my writing shine yet keeping the "Chinese flavor."

A NOTE TO THE READER

Sometimes, when things are falling apart,
they may actually be falling into place.

—*Unknown*

On an ordinary day in March of 2007, I had an early appointment with my company supervisor, Kevin, a senior vice president of a Fortune 500 company. Kevin flew in from New York for the meeting that would forever change my life.

Sitting across the room from me, Kevin said, "This is one of the most difficult decisions I have ever made. You will no longer report to me. You have a choice either to report to Nancy, who is a vice president here locally, or to look for another job elsewhere. You will need to decide within the next thirty days."

These words pierced the very fiber of my being like a sharp knife. I felt the blood draining from my head, accompanied by excruciating pain. I wanted to say, "Stop, stop. Please don't say any more." But I couldn't move my lips. Tears gushing, I felt like I was dying inside. It was so embarrassing to cry in front of Kevin. His face became fuzzy; I saw his lips moving but could no longer hear him. The next thing I remember was I was kneeling in my living room, sobbing uncontrollably.

A thought floated in my mind: *if God hadn't allowed it, this demotion from vice president to director would not have occurred. He had allowed this to happen.*

For the next few days, I locked myself in my house. Imagine hell as a place with multiple rooms of fear, sadness, anger, and hopelessness; I visited these rooms one by one. The phone rang, but I wouldn't pick up. The doorbell rang too, and someone left food baskets at my door but I only opened it when I was sure the visitors were long gone. To a background of worship music, I poured my heart and tears out as if a loved one had died. I was mourning the loss of my position as vice president.

For the first time in my life, I started to ask God, my Creator, some serious questions.

"Why has this happened to me? God, I have served You diligently for the past fifteen years. How could You let this happen to me? You have said in your Word You will bless me when I obey your commands. I have followed your commands; I give money, time, and resources to help others. Why didn't my obedience produce blessings? I am so angry at this injustice. What's more, the whole world knows I am a failure. How can I face a world that sees me as a failure? You said You loved me. How could You let such failure come upon me if You truly loved me? You promised in your Word that he who comes to You will not hunger, and he who believes in You will never thirst (John 6:35). I believed in You and your Word. But I have never been satisfied. I am still hungry and thirsty for more. Even with the title of vice president, a corner office didn't satisfy me."

I didn't hear His answers to these questions. Or maybe He did answer but I wasn't listening.

The demotion revealed the inner lens through which I was seeing God, myself, and others. I did not see God as just, as He allowed terrible things to happen in good people's lives. I saw myself as a failure and I let failure define me for a very long time.

The demotion was also the greatest awakening to my soul. Once I scraped myself up off the floor, I embarked on a journey of getting to know God for who He is, discovering who I am in Christ, and seeing others with the eyes of Jesus—a journey of returning to the Lens of Love, which is the vision God intended us to have when He created us.

The essence of this book is about letting light into our inner lens, to reveal the taints on our lenses. It is about replacing tainted lenses with the Lens of Love to usher in intimacy with God, contentment, and peace in relationships. We will focus on the mind's eye or inner vision, and how we see God, ourselves, others, and the world itself with a brand-new perspective.

For the last ten years, my dear husband and I have served as faith-based inner healing ministers to help people in the workplace and faith communities. We have witnessed powerful transformation in people's lives as they recognized the tainted lenses they see through and exchanged lies for truth, many of them setting out on a journey filled with love, joy, and peace.

Many people see God, self, and others with impaired vision. Their lenses are fashioned out of beliefs, stereotypes, lies, or judgment, with the frames of their glasses comprised of past hurts, injustices, limiting cultural beliefs, family background, generational patterns, or dysfunctions.

My heart is for people to see God, self, and others through the lens of love. I invite you to join me on a journey to discover the tainted lenses that may be clouding our vision, and toward purifying our inner vision for hope, faith, and true contentment in life.

It won't be a painless and tearless process, but the victories along the journey will be worth celebrating.

PART 1

VISION IMPAIRMENT

1
PATH OF DESTRUCTION
Failure Is a Blessing in Disguise

To crooked eyes truth may wear a wry face.

—J.R.R. Tolkien

The demotion occurred in my fifteenth year of professing to be a follower of Christ. I had been doing all the right things as a Christian: reading the Bible, participating in Sunday schools, serving as a Sunday school teacher, sharing the gospel with others through outreach, progressively giving more to the church and missions, serving the church leadership . . . you name it. And, on top of all that, I was trying to be a competent witness at my workplace by working diligently.

The demotion hit me hard as it didn't fit into my rational, logical thinking. I was taught I would be blessed when I serve and give to God. Demotion was not in any way a blessing. Yet, through the demotion, God revealed a lot of heart and soul issues in my life. For the past ten years, He has continued to guide me from the path of destruction into victory.

I grew up in a culture where there was no God. We called ourselves atheists. I grew up against a background of slogans such as "People will win against heaven," "We Chinese people are self-reliant," and "Seek truth from facts." Such sayings reflect the belief that people don't need God, and the truth is in the facts that we can see with our natural eyes and hear with our ears.

In a godless culture, logical reasoning and speculation dominate people's thought world. Believing in Jesus would be very wrong, as such a thing is for weak and irrational people only. In Romans 1:21, the Apostle Paul talks about the godless Gentiles being "futile in their thoughts" and the darkening of their foolish hearts. In other words, the eyes of their hearts became tainted or blinded. The downward spiral went like this:

From pride . . .

. . . to idolatry . . .

. . . to exchanging the truth for a lie . . .

. . . and finally, God giving people up for sexual immorality, homosexuality, and a debased mind for doing unfitting things.

It all started with "although they knew God, they did not glorify Him as God, nor were thankful . . ." (Romans 1:21 NKJV).

As an atheist, I traveled a path that led to death. As a believer who knew God yet did not glorify Him as God, I went down a road of pride and idolatry. The demotion was a wake-up call for me to see and acknowledge Him for who He is.

Questions to ponder:

+ *Do you know God?*
+ *Is your life on the path of destruction or the path of awakening?*

4

2

LACK OF VISION

A More Significant Cause of Unhappiness

Your eyes are a reflection of your spirit.

—*Unknown*

In recent years my father befriended Mr. Lin, a seventy-year-old, single, Chinese man who lives by himself. He is a fascinating man who taught history at a prominent university in China. Having immigrated to the United States in his fifties, he communicates well in English. My father, on the other hand, is a recent immigrant to the United States and still working on his English proficiency. What people may not know about Mr. Lin at first glance is he is almost completely blind. So, the friendship between the two grew out of their respective needs: my dad became Mr. Lin's eyes, and Mr. Lin became my dad's mouthpiece.

Mr. Lin's cataracts and myopia require him to read with a giant magnifier. His poor vision causes lapses in cleanliness to the extent he's received notices from the housing manager about the cockroaches and crickets originating from his apartment, causing him to be blacklisted by the apartment complex. Additionally, he relies on others to cook for him, his only alternative being staple, frozen foods. In Mr. Lin's case, as with so many others, his poor vision has significantly affected his quality of life.

A research paper entitled *The Impact of Blurred Vision on Functioning and Well-Being* published by the National Center for Biotechnology Information (Ophthalmology March 1997)[1] concluded poor vision has a more significant impact on role limitation than other physical health problems, even those such as hypertension, myocardial infarction, Type II diabetes mellitus, indigestion, urination problems, and headaches. The research was based on 1642 responders to a survey on blurred vision over a two-year period.

Similar to physical vision having a significant impact on a person's wellbeing, the inner perception (or mind's eye) has a substantial effect on a person's spiritual and emotional wellbeing.

We've all heard this phrase: it is all about one's perspective. Seeing through the mind's eye in a certain way reflects our mindset. Paul, the great teacher in the New Testament, stressed the importance of renewing our mind by shifting our perspective. He instructs believers to "Set your mind on the things above, not on the things that are on earth" (Colossians 3:2), and ". . . do not be conformed to this world, but be transformed by the renewing of your mind, so that you may prove what the will of God is, that which is good and acceptable and perfect" (Romans 12:2).

We often focus our mind on earthly things and seek to blend into or identify with the world for acceptance. God commands us to shift our perspective from earth to heaven, from the world to God, so we can see God for who He is, and see ourselves and others as He sees us, with the help of the Holy Spirit. "But we all, with open face beholding as in a glass the glory of the Lord, are changed into the same image from glory to glory, even as by the Spirit of the Lord" (2 Corinthians 3:18 KJV).

We become what we behold. When we see Jesus and make Him the focus of our vision, we will become like Jesus and walk in His ways that lead us to life, and even more abundant life. On the contrary, as King Solomon said in Proverbs, "Where there is no vision, the people are unrestrained, but happy is he who keeps the law" (Proverbs 29:18).

We live in an age where social media has become the platform for freedom of speech; the unsolicited opinions and thoughts of people fly in colorful words across the airwaves and onto our screens. Most prevalent are the negative words, which are a reflection of lawlessness. In the quote above, by "law" King Solomon was referring to God's commandments and God's words. When people lose their vision, he said, they become unrestrained. Could it be fewer people are keeping the law of God? That may lead to the rise of unhappiness.

Contentment is a rare commodity nowadays. A report in the Washington Post on March 22, 2019 stated "Life in America keeps getting more miserable," and presented the data to prove it.[2] "On a scale of 1 to 3, where 1 represents 'not too happy' and 3 means 'very happy,' Americans on average give themselves a 2.18—a hair above 'pretty happy.'"

The results show a significant decline from the happiness peak of 2.257 measured by the survey in 1993. A more than fifty percent increase in the number of people who said they're not too happy—thirteen percent in 2018 vs. eight percent in 1990—contributed to the change.

Physical vision impacts a person's wellbeing. Likewise, mental vision or spiritual eyes significantly impact a person's emotional and spiritual wellbeing. How we see God, self, and others in our mind's eye has a considerable effect on our society, community, family, and self.

In an online discussion about the meaning of *through the lens* as an idiom, Gregory Scott, a photographer, commented as follows: "It is an idiom about perspective. When you look through a lens, that lens can make things look differently. A telephoto lens makes things appear closer together. A wide angle lens gets more things in the view . . . A lens, or a filter, changes and transforms what you see. It can alter reality from the 'true' and give you a distorted or inaccurate view. Or it may help you focus on important things that otherwise you could not see. The idiom works both ways."[3]

Questions to ponder:

+ *Are you content with your life?*
+ *What is one thing you could change about your perspective for you to be more content?*

3

ORIGINAL LENS

20/20 Vision

The eyes are useless when the mind is blind.

—*Mark Venturini*

In every optometrist's office there is a universally standard vision chart, which the optometrist will use to measure your eyesight. Analogous to this universal standard eye chart, our perspective—how we see God, ourselves, and the world around us—also has a standard. These original lenses from which we get our perspective were designed by God. When our lenses deviate from the original lens, they become tainted. In this chapter, we will explore the original lens and the tainted lenses which form our perspective.

Genesis 1:26–31 tell us how, in the beginning, God made man in His image and likeness. He created man and gave him the mandate of having dominion over the creation—the fish of the sea, birds of the sky, and every living thing that moves on the earth. He blessed man to be fruitful and multiply, to fill the whole earth and subdue it.

GOD'S LENS: HIS CREATION WAS VERY GOOD

God saw His creation through His lens; He saw everything He had created was "very good." We have God's lens because He made us in His image and likeness. We can see everything He has made is "very good" when we look through His lens. And God seemed eager to invite man to see the creation as He saw it:

"And God said, 'See, I have given you every herb that yields seed which is on the face of all the earth, and every tree whose fruit yields seed; to you it shall be for food. Also, to every beast of the earth, to every bird of the air, and to everything that creeps on the earth, in which there is life, I have given every green herb for food'; and it was so. Then God saw everything that He had made, and indeed it was very good. So the evening and the morning were the sixth day" (Genesis 1:29–31 NKJV).

The history of creation reminds me of the preparation for a new baby's birth. We prepare everything they need in this world: a room, crib, monitor, bottles, clothes, blankets, even diaper genies. Gifts received at baby showers help to feather the nests we create for our newborn babies. We love our children through their conception, trimesters, delivery, and as they grow up; we never tire of looking at them through the lens of love. They look like mommy and daddy; they are loved and cherished, and they are perfect.

SEEING GOD AS WHO HE IS— A GOOD FATHER

Just as we are parents to our children, God is our Father in heaven. He has prepared everything we need to thrive and to take dominion. His words of affirmation, His provision, His purpose, and His trust all manifest His love for us. We are accepted, wanted, valued, provided for, protected, and cherished.

SEEING SELF AND OTHERS AS CHILDREN OF GOD

At the time of his creation, all man knew was God and His creation. Therefore, it is safe to conclude man only knew *good*. Through God's lens, the man saw God, himself, and all of God's creation as *good*. As a child of God, we see God as a good Father, our protector, provider, and identity affirmer. We see ourselves as loved, accepted, cherished, valued, and significant. We see others as part of the same family, as God made us all in His image.

All of this changed when Eve had a conversation with the snake in the Garden of Eden. The enemy of man's soul hijacked Adam and Eve's lenses with the temptation of lust of the flesh and pride: "'For God knows that in the day you eat from it your eyes will be opened, and you will be like God, knowing good and evil.' When the woman saw that the tree was good for food, and that it was a delight to the eyes, and that the tree was desirable to make one wise, she took from its fruit and ate; and she gave also to her husband with her, and he ate. Then the eyes of both of them were opened, and they knew that they were naked; and they sewed fig leaves together and made themselves loin coverings" (Genesis 3:5–7).

Adam and Eve's eyes were already open to see everything was *good*. In God's design, He put in us a desire to be like Him, even instructing us to be His imitators. The fulfillment of this desire is through our relationship with God. In this relationship, we see what He sees, we hear what He says, and we partner with Him in carrying out His plans for success. It is like a marriage covenant: through good times and bad times, in sickness and health, we take on the attributes of our spouse. Through our covenant relationship with God, we become like our Creator. The enemy was aware of this inbuilt desire and he offered a short cut to fulfill this desire by eating the fruit from the tree of knowledge of good and evil, which God had forbidden them.

Such was the biggest deception of all times—to sell Adam and Eve something they already had and, as a consequence, change completely the course of their and the whole of mankind's lives forever. Their dependence upon God was hacked, their communion with God broken and even unnecessary, as Satan had promised. They believed the lie that they could achieve life's purpose without God—a trap into which mankind continues to fall to this day.

After Adam and Eve ate the forbidden fruit, their eyes were opened and they knew they were naked. They suddenly saw something different from the world God had created. They no longer saw *good* but instead, they saw *shame* or maybe even *guilt* that caused them to cover up and hide their true selves with fig leaves.

After the fall, humankind took on what I call *tainted lenses*. The tainted lenses came from the lies Adam and Eve believed at the time of their fall and through which they saw themselves as being separated from God; suddenly their world was filled with fear, shame, hopelessness or death, and hatred. The terrible and ironic deception was from that point on, they had to strive to achieve whom God had already made them to be.

Before the fall, we had God's original lenses; with these lenses, our world was filled with faith, hope, and love. After the fall of humanity, how we see ourselves, God, and others, and how we want to be seen and known became tainted. Our life is a journey to return to the original lens of God, till we see our Lord face to face. "For now we see in a mirror dimly, but then face to face; now I know in part, but then I will know fully just as I also have been fully known. But now faith, hope, love, abide these three; but the greatest of these is love" (1 Corinthians 13:12–13).

The original lens—I call it the lens of love—is the original package that comes with our creation. This original lens becomes faulty, tainted, and distorted when we choose to disobey God. In our sanctification process, the Holy Spirit helps us to restore our original lens of love, enabling us to see God, self, others, and the world as *good* instead of *evil*.

TWO SETS OF LENSES

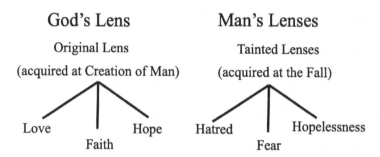

The ancient Irish hymn, *Be Thou My Vision,* translated to English in 1905,[1] describes the Lord Jesus as our vision:
"Be Thou my Vision, O Lord of my heart;
Naught be all else to me, save that Thou art.
Thou my best Thought, by day or by night,
Waking or sleeping, Thy presence my light."

Questions to ponder:

✦ *Through what lenses do you view God: lenses of love, faith, and hope, or of hatred, fear, and hopelessness?*

✦ *Through what lenses do you view yourself: lenses of love, faith, and hope, or of hatred, fear, and hopelessness?*

✦ *Through what lenses do you view others: lenses of love, faith, and hope, or of hatred, fear, and hopelessness?*

4

DO YOU FEEL HOPELESS?

Finding Jesus, Finding Hope

*But what we call our despair is often only
the painful eagerness of unfed hope.*

—George Eliot

It was during the Chinese Cultural Revolution (1966–1976); my grandparents had four sons and one daughter in their teens and twenties. One day, the local authorities took away my grandpa's shops by force. And so, my grandfather lost all means of providing for his family, the only consolation being that one of his sons worked in a government-owned shop. Despite this, the whole family suffered from hunger and starvation. My grandfather even sold his blood to buy food for his children.

Knowing this, my father and one of his brothers decided to answer the call of the government to go to one of the most remote construction areas for the promise of food. My father left Shanghai, his hometown, in 1961 for Xinjiang when he was eighteen years old. From then on, survival became a way of life for him.

Both my parents grew up in large families, and both sets of grandparents did not have good marriages. My father's parents had two different beliefs: my grandfather was a Christian and my grandmother was a Buddhist. They seemed to live apart most of the time because they could not get along. My grandfather, who was a believer, loved me although I spent very little time with him.

My mother's father was a devout Taoist. A capable carpenter, he talked about virtues, yet his actions didn't reflect much of the righteousness he preached. My grandma was the last generation of the victims of binding feet. She had six miscarriages. With her little deformed feet, she worked tirelessly to serve her husband and six children. She lived in fear—fear of losing her babies and fear of her husband's unpredictable rage—and she died in her sixties. There seemed to be a cloud of suspicion over why she died so early.

As a little girl, I was timid and insecure. My parents told me I was a chronic crier, which is not a pleasant trait for a little girl. I needed to know where my mom was and if she was alright all the time. My mom often lay in bed because of stomach pains. My dad drank a lot as part of his job during my pre-teen years. The cultural habit of making a business decision over a meal and alcohol became popular in the late 70s in China.

Every morning, my dad biked to work in another town and came home late at night. My mom went to further her medical training in another city, and this was how I found myself in charge of our household as a twelve-year-old girl. My day started with feeding the pigs and chickens, after which I would go to school. When I came home from school in the afternoon, it was time to feed the pigs and chickens again. I held my head high when my mom told her coworkers how capable I was of taking care of the household at such a young age. We sold pigs for $50 at the end of the year, which was a significant income for our family. I felt I made my parents even prouder when I handed over my score report, as I strived to get 'A' in all my subjects.

My dream was to attend a prestigious university. When I was fifteen, my family relocated to Shanghai, my dad's hometown, for business. We knew my chances of getting into an excellent high school was very slim, as I was an alien to Shanghai. I bravely asked my parents to send me back to Xinjiang to finish high school, where I would probably have a better chance to get into a good university because the quota and admission in Xinjiang were much more favorable than in Shanghai. They agreed, and I became independent at the age of fifteen. I lived by myself and cooked for myself while I went to high school for the next three years.

Such determination and effort paid off and I was selected to go to Fudan University, a well-known institution in China. Life at university was significantly different from what I'd expected. My classmates were from all over China, and they were the cream of the crop. No matter how hard I tried, I could no longer be top of my class. Looking back, it was the first significant test of my identity. I felt crushed. My worth as an excellent student was slipping away.

Since childhood, I had always allowed negativity or unpleasantness at home to affect me. Back home for my university spring break, I grabbed a bottle of hard liquor and drank up, believing death would end all the pain and despair. Three days later, lying on the floor, I heard my mother's sobs. I saw my dad come by; shaking his head, he said how stupid it was for me to end my life with a bottle of liquor, that it wouldn't change a thing. Maybe it hadn't . . . or perhaps it did change something.

One of my teachers encouraged me to go to the United States to study. This idea sparked hope in my life. Maybe living in the United States would be better. I studied English in all my free time. Eight months later, I received admission letters from several American universities. In the 1990s, the majority of student visas approved at that time were for those who applied for graduate schools with scholarships. Fortunately, I was granted a visa as an undergraduate transfer student; however, I'd have to pay for my tuition. My parents scraped together enough funds for me to study there for one year.

Many friendly people at the university welcomed international students like me. A Taiwanese family adopted me for one week while they looked for a place for me to stay. Their kindness and hospitality were overwhelming. Their two-bedroom apartment was always full of people, coming and going. The couple, Mr. and Mrs. Wu, loved and respected each other. The number of visitors didn't even seem to bother their kids. Often, people came for a meal, or worship and prayer. Jesus was the focal point of their living. I thought in my heart, this is the family life I've always wanted.

Mr. Wu invited me to watch the *Jesus* film on the last day of my stay with them. He explained the concept of sin and invited me to accept Jesus, who would forgive all of my sins. That night, I welcomed Jesus into my heart, deciding to follow God one week after my arrival in the United States. I believed He is the author of good things, and the hope for a happy family.

His salvation came to my life and filled me with hope. "And his name will be the hope of all the world" (Matthew 12:21 NLT). I quickly shared my decision with my mom over a long-distance phone call and asked her to go to church in Shanghai. She did, and soon she received the baptism. About six years later, I applied for my parents to come visit me in Arizona where I was working at the time. Due to language difficulties, they had nowhere else to go but to a Chinese church with me on Sundays. There, my father accepted Jesus. God's salvation has indeed come to my household. Today, my parents reside in the United States and are loving grandparents to my daughters.

One decision made that evening in Mr. and Mrs. Wu's loving home changed the trajectory of my life and the life of my household. The God I believe in is a God of hope. He gave me a new pair of lenses through which to view life, no longer in hopeless misery but instead with hope for a brighter future filled with light and expectation. No matter how difficult a circumstance has been in my life, the thought of suicide has never entered my mind again.

Questions to ponder:

+ *When was the last time you felt hopeless?*
+ *What is your source of hope?*
+ *Have you experienced hope when you call upon the name of Jesus?*

5

ARE YOU AFRAID?

Jesus, the Light, Dispels the Darkness of Fear

The cave you fear to enter holds the treasure you seek.

—*Joseph Campbell*

Nobody is immune to fear. Our DNA (both spiritual and physical) was altered because of sin. Fear became part of us since the fall of Adam and Eve in the Garden.

Fear was so familiar to me I could not even tell that I lived in fear much of my life. My grandma on my mother's side lived in fear. I saw my mom live in fear for most of her life until she met the Lord.

When I was six years old, I visited my maternal grandparents and was gripped by one particular fear. Many different shapes and sizes of mirrors hung outside my grandpa's room. I asked my mom why these mirrors were there and she told me grandpa used the mirrors to drive out the evil spirits. I decided there must be a lot of evil spirits as there were a lot of mirrors. I learned from my grandfather that evil spirits were powerful and could harm me.

Sometimes, my mom would take me with her to a ceremony; she would buy stacks of fake money and bring some food to the foot of a little hill outside our house. She said a prayer and burned the fake money along with incense. At that time, I never fully understood why she did that. I later learned the money was for dead family members; having received the burnt payment, they wouldn't come to trouble us. The food sacrifice was to appease the spirits so they would not come to inflict sickness on us. Our wellbeing hinged on the dead and unknown spirits floating in the air. Now I know those ceremonies were all about ancestral worship and animism.

In 2010, my husband and I had a pastor friend who invited us to join a mission trip to the Tibet Autonomous Region. What comes to mind when thinking about this Region is Mount Everest, the world's highest mountain, which is located there, and the fact that Tibetan Buddhism is deeply entrenched among the people.

Somehow, we had a heart for this city. We started to read about its people, religion, and culture, and the more we read the more our love grew for this foreign land and its inhabitants. How difficult it has always been for good news to reach this land.

One of the books we read was about the translation of the Bible into the local language, which took almost a hundred years and cost many people their lives. Reading the stories of the saints who died because they dared to share the gospel, we could almost hear the voices of the martyrs crying for the righteousness of God to rain down from heaven.

Buddhism was popular in the early '90s in the United States and there were several Buddhist Temples in Arizona. My husband and I, together with the other members of the group who would be going on the mission trip to Tibet, decided to visit a Tibetan Buddhist temple in Phoenix. I had done some research about Tibetan Buddhism on the internet and discovered there are a lot of deities for different purposes. When we arrived at the temple, we saw statues and images of the gods everywhere. Fear of the evil spirits gripped some of us, with a number complaining of headaches after the visit. In general, if we as Christians do not believe we have authority over the evil spirits, then we should avoid going to such dark places; otherwise, we may be affected by those evil spirits.

To further my preparation for the trip, I conducted a lot of research online, including finding images of the gods and spirits of the Tibetan religious beliefs. Suddenly, I heard a voice: "Look how much attention you have given me." Immediately, I stopped researching. I shared this with our friend Matthew, who had been to this land more than ten times, and he said I should delete all the research. So, I did. I hit the *Delete* button and all my research on Tibetan Buddhist gods and spirits disappeared from the screen of my computer.

A couple of months later we flew into Lhasa, Tibet's capital city, on a special visa. A giant rainbow hanging in a cloudy sky welcomed us. It was exciting to see and we were filled with expectations that His promise would be fulfilled for the people in this land. About ten of us from different parts of the world rode a bus to the Kyichu Hotel. Inside the hotel, the paintings of gods on the wall and the artifacts displayed throughout all had similar faces and feelings to the gods and spirits I had found during my online research. Every morning, noon, and afternoon, incense was offered in the hallways to the Tibetan Buddhist gods and spirits.

During one of our morning devotion times, I plucked up the courage to speak to our leader, Pastor Mark, about it.

"We are here for a mission trip," I said. "Why are we staying in this place that is full of demons and evil spirits? The images of the gods and spirits are everywhere in this hotel."

"I don't see any demons and spirits," Pastor Mark said. "All I see is Jesus."

The conviction hit me: while my eyes were focusing on demons and spirits, there was no space for Jesus. I had been so afraid of the demons and evil spirits and of what they might do to me. Why was I so frightened? Maybe, when I gazed upon these images, I had surrendered myself to the power of darkness. I had allowed fear to influence and overtake me. It was all about the focus of my eyes. When my eyes focus on Jesus, there is no space and concern for demons and evil spirits. He is love and light, the truth, the life, and the way. In the light of Jesus, all darkness has to flee.

That was *huge* for me. True freedom from fear is not in the absence of fearful objects. Instead, true freedom is when we gaze upon Jesus in the presence of fearful things. His light dispels the power of darkness.

Suddenly, a shift occurred and I was no longer concerned with the power of darkness or what it could do to me. The word I read became alive: "You are from God, little children, and have overcome them; because greater is He who is in you than he who is in the world" (1 John 4:4). With this lightning switch, I was filled with boldness to proclaim the good news of Jesus to those who had never heard about Him.

Pastor Mark is the founder of the South East Asia Prayer Center (SEAPC) and led a team of doctors, nurses, project managers, and intercessors on this particular mission trip. My husband and I were intercessors, serving a ministry called Touching Hearts. Many children in Tibet have a heart condition due to lack of oxygen in high altitudes. At a height of 12,000 feet or higher, some children's hearts do not fully develop while many others have a hole in their hearts, a condition manifested in purple lips, purple cheeks, frequent sickness, and low immunity.

Pastor Mark had prayer-walked Tibet and the Himalayan region for many years. One day, God opened a door for SEAPC to partner with the Chinese Ministry of Health to treat children with congenital heart disease. Dick Eastman's *Intercessory Worship: Combining Worship and Prayer to Touch the Heart of God* [1] tells the story of how one day, Mark sat on a bench in front of a large stone Buddha, quietly worshiping Jesus. Nearby sat a monk, reading his prayer tile. Mark began to pray for the monk, and for an opportunity to share Christ with him.

He had a gospel tract in Tibetan with him; its message about Jesus who came to live among men to sacrifice His life so all who believed might have eternal life would be foreign to a Tibetan Buddhist. Mark took the tract from his pocket and held it in the same manner the monk was holding his prayer tile. The monk looked interested, so Mark offered it to him to read. After a little while, the monk closed the tract and began weeping. Mark realized the monk had read and prayed the sinner's prayer. He put his arms around the monk who rested his face on Mark's shoulder; for several minutes the two men wept together.

Little did he know but a well-dressed Chinese officer had been watching. The officer approached and Mark wondered if he was about to be expelled from the country. Instead, the man surprised Mark by thanking him for caring for the monk. Introductions revealed that the Chinese officer was the public health director for Tibet, representing the Chinese government in Beijing. The health director asked Mark if his foundation would be interested in a health project in Tibet. Without any hesitation, Mark answered, "Yes!"

At a subsequent meeting held that same night, the health director and representatives from the People's Regional Hospital of Tibet proposed a partnership to help identify and meet the needs of children with heart defects—a common problem in Tibet. This was the door that opened as a result of Pastor Mark's walking and praying in the Himalayan heights. SEAPC established a Cath lab at a cost of millions of dollars in the city of Lhasa, treating hundreds of children over the next twelve years (2000–2012). More importantly, the families of these children received the Son of God into their hearts.

One of our activities during our mission trip was to sit with the families who anxiously awaited the outcome of heart surgery on their precious children in the SEAPC Cath lab. They once again allowed themselves to hope for a healthy child who would breathe freely in the heights of Himalaya. The promise was on the horizon: the children would no longer have purple cheeks and purple lips; they'd no longer be tied to their tents for lack of oxygen. Instead, they would be able to run freely after the mountain yaks and goats.

The families felt the presence of peace as we prayed for them and for successful surgery in the operating room. During one procedure, a child's blood pressure plunged dangerously low and the surgeon came out and asked for prayer. The child's blood pressure came back to normal shortly after the prayer, and the doctor and nurses gave glory to God in this foreign land where His name was forbidden.

Our God is love. His love is so vast. He called people like us from the other side of the world to come to this place in Tibet, 12,000 ft above the sea. We were filled with His great love to touch the hearts with holes in these people. We hugged them and embraced them even though they smelled like yak butter. God's love is deep and wide; His love reaches the people dressed in suits and ties in metropolitan cities, and His love also reaches the nomads in the heights of Himalaya.

Questions to ponder:

+ *What are you most afraid of?*
+ *When was the last time the love of God cast out fear in your life?*

6

DO YOU FEEL DISSATISFIED?

Seeing Yourself through Tainted Lenses

When you change the way you look at things,
the things you look at change.

—*Wayne Dyer*

I n 2005, in the company where I worked many people were talking about a job posting for a divisional vice president position. It was closely related to my area of expertise and as such seemed to be a good fit for my next step in the corporate world. I applied for it. Surprisingly, I was one of the few candidates on the shortlist. After many rounds of interviews with leaders locally and in New York, I received the call.

"Congratulations," the hiring manager said, "you've been selected for the position of vice president; you did well with your interviews."

My heart almost jumped out of my chest. Finally, more than ten years of hard work had paid off. It was exciting to receive this big promotion and the recognition that came with it. I'd become one of the few elites to occupy a corner office and I was one step closer to my dream of becoming a CEO. Little did I know, this promotion would lead me to where I least expected.

Being a vice president in a large organization was not as exciting as I had envisioned. The job expectation included leading teams of many talented individuals to deliver according to the plans, and to build working partnerships with business leaders across different functions. A couple of times, I realized I couldn't answer queries about technical details during conversations with senior leaders. I convinced myself that knowledge of this entry-level technical detail was not necessary for the role of vice president.

Despite this, at the year-end performance review, my leader confirmed I had performed well. The performance review included accomplishments, partnerships, and team performance. My teams had delivered according to plan, and team morale was up. As a reward, I received a bonus.

And then, in March 2007, I received the worst news of my life: demotion. It was so unexpected, it was shocking. Perhaps I had been too blind to see it coming.

With the shock came the thought that although I loved God and had diligently been doing things according to His commands, He still allowed bad things to happen in my life. I determined to stop all my doing and see if He still loved me. I asked for leave from all my duties at the church where I served. They graciously approved my request. For the next three months, I went to a different church where nobody knew me so there would be no expectations of me. I went there every Sunday and worshiped God. Every Sunday, I would immerse myself in His presence and pour out my heart and my tears. Looking back, that was when my healing journey started.

Complaining and dissatisfaction had been the norms of my life. I was blessed in so many ways and yet I couldn't see it or say it; all I could see and say was, "Not good enough. I wish I had more." My eyes were focused on the negative side of life.

Years later, a pastor friend said to me, "Your life is a life of miracles; your marriage is a miracle, your children are miracles." These words completely shifted my perspective of my life. I suddenly realized I had been looking at my life through a number of tainted lenses:

The lens of a victim: Oh, poor me. My life was full of misery and difficulties, and I'd lost my childhood to hard labor and constant worries.

The lens of an orphan: I had felt and acted like an orphan for many years, despite the fact I had a dad and a mom. My life was all up to me. I had to be independent, I had to rely on myself, and I had to work harder to provide for myself. Striving had become my standard for living.

The lens of worldly significance: My achievements and accomplishments in academia and my career gave me a sense of importance and worth. On the days when I accomplished something, I would be on a high and feel good about myself. On the days when I failed, I would feel so hopeless, as if it was the end of the world.

With these tainted lenses, my life was full of fear, anxiety, and endless toil. Even as a Christian, it wasn't easy for me to see God's goodness in my life, although I came to have a beautiful family and a husband who loves me. I always felt something was missing. When I looked at other people, I would easily spot their inadequacies, weaknesses, and areas for improvement. Likewise, I measured myself against an invisible standard and often condemned myself for falling short of that standard.

I allowed the demotion in my corporate career to define me for a long while. With time, I have learned to look at it through a different lens. With the lens of love, I came to realize failure does not define us. It only reveals us. How we see ourselves on the inside determines the life manifested on the outside. When we see ourselves as failures, then the disappointment will show up often, even if we try hard to run away from it. When we see ourselves as having no value or worth, low self-esteem and lack of confidence accompany us, even when we strive for excellence.

SEEING YOURSELF AS GOD SEES YOU

Lupita Nyong'o, a Kenyan-Mexican actress, won the Oscar for Best Supporting Actress for her role in *12 Years a Slave* (2013) at the 86th Academy Awards in 2014. Prior to her acclaimed win, Lupita addressed the ESSENCE 7th Annual Black Women in Hollywood event, saying, "I got teased and taunted about my night-shaded skin. And my one prayer to God, the miracle worker, was that I would wake up lighter-skinned. The morning would come, and I would be so excited about seeing my new skin that I would refuse to look down at myself until I was in front of a mirror because I wanted to see my fair face first. And every day I experienced the same disappointment of being just as dark as I had been the day before."[1]

She went on to say, "What is fundamentally beautiful is compassion for yourself and for those around you. That kind of beauty enflames the heart and enchants the soul."

Lupita did not see herself as God sees her. She wanted her skin color to be lighter and bleached. Like every one of us, Lupita wore tainted lenses that prevented her from seeing herself as whom God created her to be. Her success and influence in the world didn't come until she removed the self-rejection taint from her lenses. It was when she saw herself through God's lens of love that she accepted the way God created her to be.

Lupita's story from self-rejection to compassion towards herself and others is inspiring. She successfully replaced the tainted lenses of self-rejection with the lens of love to live out the second part of the greatest commandment, "Love your neighbor as yourself" (Mark 12:31). There is hope for you and me.

Questions to ponder:

+ *How do you see yourself? Do you see yourself as unique, beautiful, handsome, accepted, valuable, and significant?*

+ *How do you see God? Do you see Him as a good father, protector, and provider?*

+ *How do you see others? Do you see others as unique, valuable, and as significant as yourself?*

PART 2

THE DIAGNOSIS

7

VISIT THE OPTOMETRIST

From Physical to Spiritual— Metaphor of a Lens

*Since we cannot change reality, let us change
the eyes which see reality.*

—*Nikos Kazantzakis*

O ver the past few years, my eyes often became blurry and itchy for a short period, which I attributed to an allergy. My eyes became blurry again in December of 2018; however, this time, the blurriness and itchiness lasted for quite a long time. I realized my current contact lenses prescription had already expired. It was time to see an optometrist for an eye exam. Maybe I needed a new pair of glasses or contact lenses.

During my visit to the optometrist, I found out my near-sightedness had reduced and my farsightedness had increased. Although I hate to admit it, it seems I'm joining the reading glasses club. With a new set of contact lenses, my world became much clearer and images sharper. That is what lens correction does for us: it corrects our vision so we can see clearly.

THE ANATOMY OF AN EYE

People commonly have two eyes. Each eye has a lens—the crystal part of the eye that helps to focus light or an image on the retina. The lens has a similar function to the lens of a camera, while the retina is the light-sensitive tissue at the back of the eye. The lens needs to be clean and clear for the retina to receive a sharp image. When the light focuses on the retina, you will have 20/20 vision. The amount of light able to penetrate the lens and reach the retina reflects the health of an eye.

Nearsightedness is a condition where close objects appear clearly, while far away objects appear blurry.[1] This occurs because the light focuses in front of the retina.

Farsightedness is a condition where close objects appear blurry, while far away objects appear clearly.[2] It occurs when the light penetrates too far, causing it to focus past the retina.

The causes of nearsightedness and farsightedness include the distorted shape of the eyeball, cornea, or lens.

Astigmatism is a condition in which the eye does not focus light evenly on the retina.[3] A healthy eye has a basketball-like cornea, with the same degree of roundness in all areas. An eye with astigmatism has a cornea that is curved more like a football, with some areas steeper or more rounded than others. This can cause images to appear blurry and stretched out. All three of the above defects of the eye cause imperfect vision and need correction to see clearly.

The lens of an eye consists mostly of water and protein. Another defect is when the protein clumps up, clouding the lens and reducing the light reaching the retina, forming a cataract. Further, as we age, our lenses become dull and insensitive to focus. We need glasses to correct the vision so we can see from far and near with almost or absolute 20/20 vision.

Much like me, you might have visited an optometrist for an eye exam. The reason for your visit was that you wanted to see clearly. The typical optometrist visit includes:

1. A questionnaire about you and your family's health history and history of eye problems.

2. Evaluation of your vision using a standard eye chart.

3. Identification of defects and the degree of the impairment (nearsightedness, farsightedness, astigmatism, cataract, etc.).

4. Prescription for vision correction.

5. New lens/glasses fitting.

The questionnaire can help to identify possible root causes of eye disease, while various eye exams help to diagnose any defects. You then order either glasses or contact lenses, or perhaps may be required to have surgery. With your new lenses, you will be able to see much more precisely, near and far. The world is no longer blurry and the people in front of you are no longer shadows.

Like our physical lens, we have a spiritual lens that serves as a filter in viewing God, others, and self. We were created with the lens of love to be able to receive the light fully without hindrance. God is light and He is the truth, the way, and the life (John 14:6). As we age, our spiritual lenses become tainted by such things as our past, generational traits, cultural background, and beliefs. With examination, we can discover what has tainted our spiritual lenses and then work to replace them with the lens of love so we can see God, others, and ourselves with fresh, new vision.

Questions to ponder:

+ *When was the last time you had a spiritual vision exam?*
+ *What could be a possible diagnosis of your spiritual vision exam through the lens of love?*

+ *What are the symptoms of your spiritual vision problem, if any?*
+ *Who in your family line may have tainted lenses?*
+ *What are some of the tainted lenses in your family line— on both paternal and maternal sides?*

8

TAINTED LENSES—A SPIRITUAL PERSPECTIVE

Returning to the Lens of Love

You have the ability to adjust the lens through which you view the world.

—Jeffrey G. Duarte

Just like visiting an optometrist for an eye exam and obtaining glasses or contact lenses, there is a process for a spiritual eye exam and receiving a clear lens of love. Imagine you are going to see Jesus, our greatest Physician, for a spiritual eye exam. The process may look something like this:

1. A questionnaire about you and your family's spiritual lens history and the history of your tainted lenses (see below).

2. Evaluation of your current lenses against the lens of love (see below).

3. Identification of your spiritual vision impairment and tainted lenses (see Chapters 9 and 10).

4. Prescription for lens correction (see Part 3).

5. Benefits of seeing life through the lens of love (see Part 4).

QUESTIONNAIRE

Throughout this book, you will find questions that you may ponder to help identify any tainted lenses or impairment of spiritual eyesight you and your family line may have. In addition, at the end of this book you will find a questionnaire that will help you further assess any tainted lenses you may have. I encourage you to find a quiet place, sit alone with the Lord, and ask the Holy Spirit to scan your spiritual vision. He will reveal any tainted lenses you have as well as those passed down from your family line as you consider and answer these questions.

LENS EVALUATION

In Chapter 3, I defined the lens of love as the lens of God. When we measure our lenses against the lens of love, we will know whether or not our lenses have taints or impurities. As an example, let's look at how I examined the lenses with which I view God, self, and others.

My lens in viewing God

There is an increasing measure of clarity in my lens in seeing God over time. When I was an atheist, my lens in seeing God was solid black. As the Apostle Paul wrote, ". . . the god of this world has blinded the minds of the unbelieving so that they might not see the light of the gospel of the glory of Christ, who is the image of God" (2 Corinthians 4:4). As an atheist, I was spiritually blind.

My lens for seeing God became clearer after I accepted Jesus into my heart. It was no longer solid black, but I saw Him as a stone-faced father figure. My view of God came more from head knowledge than heart connection and experience. God blessed me in my work and ministry—I was the head and not the tail. Looking back, I was devoted, obedient, and blessed but not yet content. At that time, I believed He blessed me because I was a good girl. This perceived conditional love kept me on the performance treadmill. I continued to live my life without dying completely to myself (my worldly ambitions and pride). I had a partially covered lens, and the God I saw was only part of who He really is.

I experienced a dry spiritual season right before my demotion in early 2007; I hungered for more of God. I knew everything that was going on in my life could not satisfy me. There had to be more. The hunger and thirst led me to ask for prayer from a pastor in a church where the gifts of the Holy Spirit were allowed to operate fully. After an encounter with the Holy Spirit, my prayer life started to change—and so did my understanding and view of God.

Then the demotion in my workplace made room for me to really examine the taints in my lenses. I came to the point where I can confidently say that my God is a good Father who delights in having me sit on His lap and showing me His plans.

My love for God continues to increase as the lens through which I view God becomes clearer. Also, I became more willing to die to myself. Jesus set an example for the greatest love by laying down His life. "There is no greater love than to lay down one's life for one's friends" (John 15:13 NLT).

Increasing love for God reflects fewer taints in our lenses for seeing God and shows we are moving closer to the lens of love.

My lens in viewing self

A. W. Tozer, the author of the classic devotional, *The Knowledge of the Holy*, is quoted as saying, "What comes into our minds when we think about God is the most important thing about us."[1] How we see God is the foundation of how we see ourselves.

When I was an atheist, I saw myself as an ugly duckling through the tainted lens with which I viewed myself. I refused to go to the physical education class during my first year of college. Everyone had to wear a swimsuit for that class. I didn't own a swimsuit and never wanted to show that much skin to others. Perhaps I was afraid of the water or ashamed of my body but I preferred to take the penalty for missing that class than show myself in a swimsuit.

After I became a believer, my self-esteem started to improve. In early 2000, after I'd been working for a few years, I decided to buy a house. My realtor was very complimentary. "Look at you," she said, "I wish my daughter was like you. You've got everything together; you have a good job; you travel around the world. Now you're getting a house on your own." Her words affirmed my self-perception: *Hey, I'm doing pretty good. I'm successful.* Subtly, this sense of success led me to a false image of my importance.

The demotion smashed my false image of importance. The brokenness from the demotion and the healing that followed brought me to see my true value as a precious daughter of God—without strings attached. The lens through which I see myself now is not completely untainted but I am on a journey to return to the point of seeing myself through the lens of love.

The book of Romans tells us, "God has given me grace to speak a warning about pride. I would ask each of you to be emptied of self-promotion and not create a false image of your importance. Instead, honestly assess your worth by using your God-given faith as the standard of measurement, and then you will see your true value with an appropriate self-esteem" (Romans 12:3 TPT).

My lens in viewing others

French artist Marc Chagall (1887–1985) said, "In our life there is a single color, as on an artist's palette, which provides the meaning of life and art. It is the color of love."

One afternoon in 2013, I looked out of an upstairs window of our home to see my husband arrive in a taxi, accompanied by another man whom I didn't know. My husband waved at me and asked me to join them downstairs in the living room.

"This young man, Ibrahim, has severe back pain," he said. "Let's pray for him."

My husband got the impression that Ibrahim might have uneven legs. Sure enough, on a closer look we noticed his right leg was a bit shorter than the left one. His right leg responded to our prayer and started to grow longer in front of our eyes. It stopped growing when both legs were aligned. To his amazement, Ibrahim stood up and twisted at the waist from side to side, and there was no more pain in his back. He was so excited. He asked if he could bring his wife, Zaina, for prayer the next day. Of course, we said yes.

After he'd left, my husband explained to me that Ibrahim was from Iraq. There, he had been a successful soccer player but came to the United States as a refugee, looking for a better life. His wife couldn't conceive, which was why he wanted to bring her for prayer the next day.

It was a Sunday afternoon when this young couple drove up to our house and jumped out of the car. Zaina was a beautiful young lady with a hajib covering her head. For the next thirty minutes, we were led by the Holy Spirit to pray with her to release bitterness and unforgiveness towards her family members and towards herself. We blessed this couple and prayed that God would give them the gift of life and open her womb. They left and we didn't hear from them again for a while.

A year later, we'd moved to Hong Kong and forgotten about this incident when one day, my husband received a phone text from Ibrahim, with a picture of a baby. "Do you remember me?" the text read. "The boy in the picture is my son. You prayed for us to have children. He is now one month old. Thank you for praying."

Father God's goodness blew us away—He had granted this couple's miracle, despite their different beliefs about Him. We were so excited to be a part of this miracle. Before, I used to see people like Ibrahim and Zaina with tainted lenses, such as "Surely, they wouldn't accept prayer from someone like me, a Christian woman." But then I heard God's still, small voice: "You must see them with My lens of Love."

Although this wonderful young couple were of a different "religion" they could taste the goodness of Father God and see Him for who He truly is—the One who gives good gifts and who loves them. Regardless of backgrounds and beliefs, He is ultimately the Father who loves all creation and wants all to come to the knowledge of the Truth.

Our inner lenses are tainted by our family history and generational patterns. Our perception of past experiences and significant events in our lives can also affect our lenses. Perhaps that is why the Apostle Paul commands us, "And do not be conformed to this world, but be transformed by the renewing of your mind, so that you may prove what the will of God is, that which is good and acceptable and perfect" (Romans 12:2).

The world around us can influence our inner lenses and thus draw us away from seeing through the lens of love, which is good and acceptable and perfect.

We will now examine a few of the possible causes of tainted lenses, and how those taints may manifest themselves.

Questions to ponder:

✦ *When was the last time you experienced the lens shift in seeing God, self, and others?*

✦ *Have your lenses through which you see God, self, and others become clearer over time?*

9

TAINTED LENSES—
A HISTORICAL PERSPECTIVE

1: Family History & Generational Patterns

*Seeing unhealthy patterns in your family and deciding that
those patterns end with you and will not be passed down
to future generations, is an extremely brave and
powerful decision.*

—Tiny Tot (The Minds Journal)

When we go to the doctor's office, we are often asked about our family history regarding sickness and disease. The common belief is that physical weakness and illness could pass down from one generation to another. If a family has a history of vision problems or eye disease, the patient may be prone to have those same problems or diseases.

Parallel to this generational pattern in physical attributes is a generational pattern in spiritual traits that may pass from one generation to the next. A good example of this pattern is

Abraham and his son Isaac as their stories are told in Genesis, the first book of the Bible.

Abraham's wife, Sarah, was very beautiful. When he came to settle in a new land, he was afraid her beauty would cost him his life, so he decided they would tell others she was his sister. "Abraham said of Sarah his wife, 'She is my sister.' So Abimelech king of Gerar sent and took Sarah" (Genesis 20:2). This was a half-truth as Sarah was indeed the daughter of Abraham's father with a different mother; however, he omitted to tell the truth that Sarah was also his wife.

Abraham's son, Isaac, repeated the same pattern. "When the men of the place asked about his wife, he said, 'She is my sister,' for he was afraid to say, 'my wife,' thinking, 'the men of the place might kill me on account of Rebekah, for she is beautiful'" (Genesis 26:7).

Abraham told a white lie to protect himself but this almost cost him his marriage and very nearly aborted God's promise of seed by faith until God intervened. Isaac told exactly the same lie to protect himself. Both Abraham and Isaac had a lens of fear of man.

Whether we like it or not, we inherit certain traits from our family line. A grandmother who struggled with abuse and a victim mindset sees her daughter and even her granddaughter fall into abusive relationships and become victims themselves. Likewise, tainted lenses can also pass from one generation to another. Hope in Christ is to recognize these and bring them to Jesus for redemption—He will exchange them for the lens of love. He certainly has done that for my family.

In the next two sections, I will share a few sets of tainted lenses that became evident in my family line.

Questions to ponder:

✦ *Can you identify any dysfunctional generational patterns in your family line and your life?*

✦ *Do you recognize or pinpoint how these patterns may affect your life in a negative way?*

✦ *Do you think they are hindering you from living an abundant life?*

LENS OF FEAR OF DEATH

In a small house on top of a mountain in western China, a pregnant woman was about to give birth. There was no hospital or medical facility nearby. Cows, goats, and sheep grazed the mountain slope for food during the warm seasons. But on this, the last day of the year, the bitter wind and snow kept the few families and all their animals inside. The pregnant woman's mother had come from far away to help her daughter during the last weeks of her pregnancy and through her labor. But things didn't go entirely according to plan.

"Mum, my water's broken. Give me a towel." The two women stared at each other in shock. The pregnant woman sat in a pool of water, stunned by this turn of events. Her mother, with ashen face and quivering lips, looked as if she'd seen a ghost. A short while later, the pregnant woman pushed and the baby came out into the world, six weeks earlier than expected.

A telegram was sent to the baby's father, asking him to come home from his work assignment to be with his wife and first child. Days passed by. There was no response or even a shadow of the father.

The child was welcomed into this world by her mother and her grandmother, who wasn't in any emotional state to truly embrace her.

I was that baby girl.

Much later in my life, mom told me grandma had lost six babies during childbirth. That explained why she went into shock and was unable to function when my mom gave birth to me. The trauma of childbirth had brought much fear to my maternal grandparents. My grandfather turned to Taoism for protection. Taoists believe people can become deities or live forever by practicing certain rituals and asceticism. Taoists are always looking for herbs or concoctions to take away their sickness and disease so they can achieve immortality. My grandfather did not achieve immortality and died in his eighties. My grandmother passed away in her 60s.

My mom's family passed down the lens of fear of death.

Life is full of anxiety when you see it through the lens of fear of death. The body becomes the head of the whole being; soul and spirit are secondary. In their striving for immortality, whenever there is a pain in a particular part of the body, Taoists believe an imbalance of the elements has obstructed the flow of energy and caused the pain. The remedy is to use elixirs to remove the obstruction by adding specific elements and reducing other elements to restore balance. They believe health is in a person's own hands and also at the mercy of all the gods in nature.

Even after I became a believer, the lens of fear of death plagued my life, manifesting in my life as an excessive concern for my younger daughter's health. She was born with some digestion issues: a gassy stomach that was easily irritated. Sometimes, I would have to push the stroller around the house endlessly to help her go to sleep. When she turned three months old, we took her to see a natural doctor and found out she had a bunch of food allergies.

I felt like I was walking on eggshells during her early years as we discovered to what she was and wasn't allergic. She loved strawberries and ate a lot, but the bright red strawberries contributed to her digestive upset and we found out later she was allergic to anything red. When she was two years old, I took her with me to get flu shots, with the best intention of protecting us both from getting the flu. Instead of strengthening us, it was the start of a respiratory nightmare that lasted six months. She would frequently throw up and cough non-stop. Many times, I rushed to daycare to pick her up after a throw-up episode. A year later, we found out she and I were among the few who cannot receive flu shots—rather than strengthening and protecting us, the shot severely weakened our immune systems.

When COVID-19 broke out in the United States in the March of 2020, people were afraid for their lives. One day, our older daughter said, "My friends' parents are terrified of being infected with COVID-19. Only my parents aren't afraid at all."

This observation spoke of the progress I have made towards increasing freedom from the lens of fear of death. The good news is that Jesus has already defeated the devil who had the power of death and set us free from slavery to the fear of death. "Therefore, since [these His] children share in flesh and blood [the physical nature of mankind], He Himself in a similar manner also shared in the same [physical nature, but without sin], so that through [experiencing] death He might make powerless (ineffective, impotent) him who had the power of death—that is, the devil—and [that He] might free all those who through [the haunting] fear of death were held in slavery throughout their lives" (Hebrews 2:14–15 AMP).

We may be sick and we will die one day, but we don't have to be haunted by the fear of death. As Dwight L. Moody said, "Death may be the King of terrors . . . but Jesus is the King of kings!"

Questions to ponder:

+ *Do you think you have the lens of the fear of death?*
+ *Can you identify how this fear may have been passed down to you through your family line?*

LENSES OF HATRED AND INJUSTICE

As a young man, my father was always hungry. There was never enough food in their house. The authorities had forcefully taken my grandfather's grain business and two successful shops without any explanation. With that, the family's means of making ends meet disappeared. How could my grandfather feed his five children? Each morning, grandfather would pour out his bitterness and resentment for such cruel injustice to God in heaven.

One day, everyone in the neighborhood was talking about an announcement made by the government. They were promising enough food to eat for anyone willing to go to a new territory in western China—cows, sheep, goats, and endless land that people would be able to plant and harvest for food. It was a veritable land of milk and honey. The government would send the willing pioneers to the area by train, where they could establish new homes.

The images of meat, rice, corn, and wheat bread floated in the family's minds. Any day when they had something with which to fill their stomachs was a good day. They knew their father was eating rice bran in secret and saving rice for his young, growing children. Those were lean and hopeless times . . . until the news of this new land of opportunity.

Two of the brothers stood up and told their father, "We will go to this new territory to get food and make a living. We will send money back to you—a portion of our salaries."

Their father agonized for several days over this impossible decision: to let his sons go to this remote place, thousands of miles away, or keep them starving at home? Finally, he gave them his tearful approval. He didn't know at the time one of his beloved sons would be forever gone.

My father was eighteen years old when he left with his brother for a better life in the new territory. A few years passed. The two brothers worked hard; at least they had enough food

49

to eat, and true to their promise, they were able to send some money back to their father.

The new territory was nothing like the big city where they had grown up. The snow-covered winter seemed to be very long. My uncle lived in the north part of the new territory, where there were cold water fish in the rivers. He wanted his brother to join him there so he could eat fish instead of potatoes. One year, during the springtime when the snow and ice were melting, he went to catch some fish on a raft. Somehow, his log raft flipped over. The water was so freezing he died in that cold river. My father, for the first time in his life, took an airplane ride to bury his brother after receiving a telegram with the devastating news.

My father couldn't bring himself to tell my grandfather his son had died in the new territory. My grandfather found out about the tragedy one year later. He wept and shouted. He had lost his businesses, and now his beloved son.

Trauma can taint our lenses on many levels. We have already looked at how tainted lenses are a spiritual condition affecting our relationship with God, self, and others. Tainted lenses can also negatively affect our health.

Two sets of lenses were passed on from my father's side to me: the lens of hatred and the lens of injustice.

We know a tree is good or bad by examining its fruit. "Either make the tree good and its fruit good, or make the tree bad and its fruit bad; for the tree is known by its fruit" (Matthew 12:33). When a person sees himself through the lens of hatred, so self-hatred, regret, guilt, and self-criticism constantly plague his mind and he feels small, unworthy, and hopeless.

When a person sees God through the lens of hatred, trust in God or any authority figure is almost an impossibility. Instead, the person opts for "independence." Sooner or later, however, this person finds himself in a hot mess due to dishonoring and disrespecting any leader, for example by pointing out their

shortcomings. The result is often fear due to broken relationships, and fear frequently manifests itself physically in disease.

When a person sees others through the lens of hatred, he
is easily offended and prone to carry or hold on to offenses.
Somehow, the person holding onto the offense believes that
this will punish the offender; in reality, it puts the offended
person in a prison of bitterness and unforgiveness. It's common knowledge that unforgiveness is one of the leading causes
of many diseases.

The Bible says hatred blinds people. "But the one who
hates his brother is in the darkness and walks in the darkness,
and does not know where he is going because the darkness has
blinded his eyes" (1 John 2:11). Martin Luther King, Jr. said,
"Darkness cannot drive out darkness; only light can do that.
Hate cannot drive out hate; only love can do that."

When a person sees the world with the lens of injustice,
he tends to seek revenge in his own way. My grandfather used
words as his tool of revenge. He would tell whoever had ears
to listen about the terrible things that had happened to him
and his family. My grandfather was diagnosed with colon
cancer in his 70s. I believe his bitter words of revenge affected
his digestion but by the grace of God, he lived another ten
years into his 80s.

As for me, I viewed my demotion as a grave injustice
because of the tainted lenses in my family line.

Questions to ponder:

+ *Do you have the lens of hatred?*
+ *Do you have the lens of injustice?*
+ *Can you identify how the lenses of hatred and injustice
  may have been passed down to you through your family
  line?*

2: Personal Experience

We all get so caught up in the moment of what we're doing every day, it's hard to hit that reset button and get pulled away from all that and see life from a different perspective.

—*Tony Stewart*

In our lives, one event can change our lives forever. For David in the Bible, it was slaying the giant, Goliath. For Paul, it was being blinded by the light of Jesus on the road to Damascus. For Peter, it was catching the netful of fish when he met Jesus after a whole night of vain effort. These events forever altered the path of their lives.

Demotion forever changed the trajectory of my life. If it were not for my demotion, I would have continued chasing positions and titles to prove my significance in the world. I would have continued to serve God as a responsible child but with an unfulfilled desire for deep intimacy.

I thought I was on the journey of pursuing God. Somehow, He still seemed far away. The demotion hit a reset button. I knew my life couldn't continue the way it had up to that point. Isaiah 55:8–9 in particular spoke to me: "'For My thoughts are not your thoughts, nor are your ways My ways,' declares the Lord. 'For as the heavens are higher than the earth, so are My ways higher than your ways and My thoughts than your thoughts.'"

My quest for His thoughts and His ways began. It was kind of late for this quest to start after fifteen years as a believer. Oh well, it's better to live in peace than to live in regret. I had to believe it was never too late to seek His thoughts and His ways.

My heart continually yearned for intimacy with my Creator and my Lord. Over the decade following the demotion, I discovered some tainted lenses that hindered me from walking closely with the Lord. In the next few sections, I will discuss the lenses of idolatry, pride, ungodly expectation, and the past. It is my prayer that sharing my journey and discoveries will be a blessing and a help to you on your own journey of discovery.

LENS OF IDOLATRY

A few months after my demotion, I shared my ordeal with a fellow attendee who went to the same *Waiting on God* retreat. After hearing about my corporate journey from promotion to demotion, he said, "I know what's happened to you." I leaned forward, eager to hear what he had to say. "Your job title and position has become an idol in your heart, and this idol has enslaved you."

What? I was shocked by what I heard. Idolatry is a word I hear in church and it even has one of the Ten Commandments dedicated to it. How can I be breaking one of those Ten Commandments? I'd never heard reference to it in the business world.

America is a land where people have the freedom to pursue and fulfill their dreams. The dream typically includes a successful career, a big house with a white picket fence, cars, happy vacations, and so on. All along, as an immigrant from China, I'd believed I was pursuing the *American Dream*.

The Google dictionary definition for an idol is an image or representation of a god used as an object of worship. Maybe unconsciously, I believed a particular title or position would prove my worth and significance. I'd always dreamed of being the CEO of a company. Like many of my colleagues, I'd worked hard to climb up the corporate ladder. Entry-level analyst, manager, director, vice president, executive vice president, senior vice president, president, group president, and then, CEO—that is the career path for those who are willing to sacrifice their life to the pursuit of it.

It is not wrong to pursue our dreams. For a believer, such pursuit outside of God and without God is in danger of becoming idolatry. Author, coach, and speaker, A.R. Bernard, tweeted, "Idolatry is seeking security and meaning in someone or something other than God."[1]

Sometimes, our strong desire for something overrides God's will or we turn a deaf ear to God's voice. Maybe that is why the Bible calls it *evil desire*. "Behold, the man who would not make God his refuge, but trusted in the abundance of his riches and was strong in his evil desire" (Psalm 52:7). We are called to die to this kind of evil desire as it leads to idolatry. "Therefore consider the members of your earthly body as dead to immorality, impurity, passion, evil desire, and greed, which amounts to idolatry" (Colossians 3:5).

Idolatry is a form of worship and a matter of the heart. "The idols of the nations are but silver and gold, the work of man's hands. They have mouths, but they do not speak; they have eyes, but they do not see; they have ears, but they do not hear, nor is there any breath at all in their mouths. Those who make them will be like them, yes, everyone who trusts in them" (Psalm 135:15–18). Opposite of an idol, God speaks, God sees, God hears, God breathes, and God moves.

King David is praising God as the one and only true God in Psalm 135:13: "Your name, O Lord, is everlasting, Your remembrance, O Lord, throughout all generations." The nations did not worship God; they worshipped the idols of materialism, achievement, and accomplishment by human effort. Idols are dumb (*they have mouths, but do not speak*), blind (*they have eyes, but do not see*), deaf (*they have ears, but do not hear*), and lifeless (*there is no breath at all in their mouths*). And, King David warns, people who worship idols become like them: dumb, blind, deaf, and lifeless.

Like me, your initial reaction to this passage may be, "I can speak, see, hear, and breathe. There is no such thing as an idol in my heart." However, I believe the dumb, blind, deaf, and lifeless attributes refer to our connection with God. When I idolize a certain position or job title, I strive to obtain my worth, value, and significance from that. As long as you have an idol in your heart, some aspects of dumbness, blindness, deafness, and lifelessness will manifest in your life.

When we see God through the lens of idolatry, we are blind to God's love. "Those who cling to worthless idols turn away from God's love for them" (Jonah 2:8 NIV). When I was serving the idol of accomplishment, I was blind to God's unconditional love. My ability in hearing God and obtaining Bible knowledge was limited. My ear was not tuned into His divine guidance but rather inclined to the wisdom for worldly success. Looking back, I was busy being a Christian with little room in me for His guidance, His ways, and His glory.

When we see ourselves through the lens of idolatry, we often see ourselves as slaves to the idol in exchange for a better life but end up with empty promises. "However at that time, when you did not know God, you were slaves to those which by nature are no gods" (Galatians 4:8).

When we have an idol in our hearts our spiritual lens is tainted or even blind, and our understanding towards God becomes dull. The book of Isaiah tells us a person who makes and worships idols cannot see and their hearts cannot understand. "And the rest of it he makes into a god, His carved image. He falls down before it and worships it, prays to it and says, 'Deliver me, for you are my god!' They do not know nor understand; for He has shut their eyes, so that they cannot see, and their hearts, so that they cannot understand" (Isaiah 44:17–18 NKJV).

The demotion exposed my tainted lenses of idolatry. Looking back at my corporate life, I was like a madwoman running a hundred miles per hour in the pursuit of success, hoping the desired position and title would do the trick and give me what, in fact, only God could give me. If it were not for the demotion, I would have continued on this endless quest. One day, I would feel the excitement and pride of accomplishment; the next day, disappointment would set in. Maybe the next ladder, or the next . . . I gave all my strength, heart, and soul to this relentless chase, regardless of my health, my rest, and my family.

Idolatry takes and takes; you can never satisfy it. Little did I know but it consumed my time, my mind, and my strength. My love, affection, and devotion to this idol were only evident to me when the position and title were no longer there.

One and half years after I accepted the demotion and successfully built up a new team, I decided to resign from my job and focus on my family. I thought since I'd have "more time" now, I would learn to wait on the Lord. Every time, the *wait* turned to a sweet snooze. Day after day, month after month, I kept falling asleep when I waited on the Lord. Maybe I was trying to make up from overworking in my previous corporate job; maybe I'd lost who I was.

My work, accomplishment, rewards, position, and titles had always made who I was and had become my identity. Suddenly, once I gave up the job and the sense of accomplishment, I didn't know who I was anymore. That is what idolatry does to people: while we are busy serving the idol, we become enslaved to that idol and we lose our true identity as children of God.

My idol was accomplishment, along with the accompanying titles and positions. For you, the idol could be something different. I have seen people idolize a platform, approval from specific authority figures, spiritual gifts, children, spouses, a particular lifestyle, fame, social media following and likes, a circle of people they are associated with, financial security, or status.

Another typical idol is *self*: I can do whatever I want, whenever I want, and how I want; I am in control of my life. People live a life as if God doesn't exist or care. Even Christians are not immune to self-idolatry. Self-idolaters live in the "me, myself, and I" unholy trinity. Becoming intimate and one with

God is out of reach for self-idolaters as they cannot serve two masters at the same time.

The wisdom from God's Word is "But seek first His kingdom and His righteousness, and all these things will be added to you" (Matthew 6:33). When we love and seek God, His kingdom, and righteousness as our priority, there is a natural by-product. "The blessing of the Lord brings wealth, without painful toil for it" (Proverbs 10:22 NIV).

In summary, we lose our true identity as a child of God when the lenses of idolatry taint our eyes and when our identity is tied to our accomplishments and performance through striving and work. We became prideful because of our efforts. Unfortunately, life becomes hopeless as the work is never enough.

To rid ourselves of the lens of idolatry, we first need to recognize the idols in our heart. At the prompting of the Holy Spirit, we can examine our connection with God. Is our connection with God life-flowing where He speaks, we hear; He breathes, we receive the infilling of the Holy Spirit; He shows, we see; and He moves, we follow; or is it a lifeless, pseudo connection? Lack of understanding and experience of God's unconditional love may expose the tainted lens of idolatry.

May we know our God, the one and only God. "I am the Lord, and there is no other; besides Me there is no God. I will gird you, though you have not known Me; that men may know from the rising to the setting of the sun that there is no one besides Me. I am the Lord, and there is no other" (Isaiah 45:5–6).

And may we come to know Him as He really is—a good Father. "Listen to Me, O house of Jacob, and all the remnant of the house of Israel, you who have been borne by Me from birth and have been carried from the womb; even to your old age I will be the same, and even to your graying years I will bear you! I have done it, and I will carry you; and I will bear you and I will deliver you" (Isaiah 46:3–4).

Questions to ponder:

✦ *Is your connection with God life-flowing?*

✦ *What does God's unconditional love look like to you?*

✦ *Does your profession or occupation define who you are?*

✦ *Is your worth defined by what you do or who you are?*

LENS OF PRIDE

The demotion was a lightning-strike experience for me. My tainted lenses and blindness were exposed. Once the shocking news of my demotion had sunk in, I'd calmed down and begun to come to terms with it, I spent a lot of time on the phone and internet in a desperate search to find a new job within thirty days. I agonized over the different possibilities: to accept the demotion and stay at the same company, or to leave altogether for another job in a different company.

The prospect of making another mistake was frightening. The thought of failure paralyzed me. As time passed by, none of the job opportunities outside of my company worked out, but even so, I was determined to stay in the same city. A few months later, I found out why I had to stay in the same town—God had a much better plan for my life.

In my native culture, demotion is shameful. No one wants to *lose face*, and so they will do anything to maintain the appearance they have it all together: they are in control, superior, and successful; they have status and money, and everything else that goes with that.

Shame follows you around when you lose face. While merely thinking about going back to my workplace with a lower-level position, I could imagine the disappointment and pity in people's eyes. I could feel the negative energy from my coworkers hovering above me like my raincloud.

As I stood at this crossroads, some leaders, mentors, and friends took the time to talk with me. I appreciate their advice and wisdom to this day. During a transition, having friends whom you can trust and pour your heart out to is a huge blessing. Two of my mentors advised me to take the demotion and continue my career. At that time, however, taking the demotion required more courage than quitting.

Finally, I surrendered. I surrendered my pursuit for a vice president position in other companies. I abandoned all my efforts to "save face" and create the illusion I had it all together. I surrendered to God's ways. You could say I was reluctantly obedient because I didn't feel I had much choice. Although fear gripped me, I gathered the courage to face the perceived disappointment from my coworkers and leaders. I accepted the demotion and started to work locally for a new leader.

Often, we make up a whole world out of the fear in our minds—a world that is unpredictable, unknown, that may bite and be painful. It is so frightening that we resist this world with all our strength. But actually—once we cross the chicken line—we discover this world isn't as bad as we imagined.

This was my discovery once I returned to work. Soon, I found out my demotion wasn't the end of the world. In my new role as director of a new and dysfunctional team, I was able to provide value to this team who were beaten up and low in morale. I listened to and heard their frustration and disappointment. Setting up a strategy to rebuild the team, I interviewed and recruited many more members to alleviate their heavy workload. The team's morale improved greatly because, at last, they felt the leadership heard them and cared for them. Their contributions were recognized and rewarded. They were productive, delivered results, and became a high performing team. For me, it was an invaluable lesson in humility, as I learned to get off my high horse, view others as equally valuable as myself, and take action to provide leadership and real value.

Where we position ourselves affects our perspective. It's like hiking: there is the exhilaration of surveying the world when we reach the top. The panoramic view may be worth the hard work of the uphill climb. When we stand at the summit, we look down; the other hikers, slowly moving up along the trail, look so small. It's easy to forget that, a little while ago, we were down there too. Standing on the top doesn't make us superior, simply because we have a better view. Unfortunately, this is the way the world sees it: people who live in houses with spectacular views of the ocean or mountains are better than those who don't have any view at all.

Pride's foundation is self-effort and works. There is perceived differentiation in the amount, levels, degree of effort, and the works themselves. As soon as we enter the comparison mode, pride is in full effect. When we don't know our true identity, pride clothes us with a false identity based on our achievement and works.

Pride blocks our vision and limits our learning and growth. It is an arrogant view of ourselves based on our accomplishments. I loved to receive compliments from people:

"Wow, you're so capable."

"You are one of the youngest people we know to have a Ph.D."

"You have a corner office."

"You travel around the world for work."

"You've gotten everything together."

These words and other similar compliments were music to my ears and pushed me to work harder to maintain my superior status. The danger is that, often, we start to look down on those people who don't seem to have achieved so much.

Everyone seemed to be climbing the corporate ladder tirelessly. Only one or two of my colleagues willingly gave up their promotion in favor of lower-level positions because they were a better fit. I now really admire those exceptional people who didn't bow down to the cultural norm of climbing the corporate ladder. They didn't need to; they knew who they were. I came to truly understand one of King Solomon's pearls of wisdom: "It's better to wait for an invitation to the head table than to be sent away in public disgrace" (Proverbs 25:7 NLT).

One of the best-known characters in the Bible who walked down the ladder from pride to humility was the Apostle Paul. He too had a lightning-strike moment, so much so he was literally struck blind.

The story went like this: Saul was highly educated and a Pharisee. The Pharisees believed attaining righteousness could only be done by observing the Law. Their teaching demanded Jews should obey all 600+ laws in the Torah and oral traditions. Saul took great pride in his religious practice for he had been "circumcised the eighth day, of the nation of Israel, of the tribe of Benjamin, a Hebrew of Hebrews; as to the Law, a Pharisee; as to zeal, a persecutor of the church; as to the righteousness which is in the Law, found blameless" (Philippians 3:5–6).

One of the possible reasons why Saul persecuted Christians was that these Christ-followers proclaimed Jesus was the Messiah, the anointed one who would save the Jews from their oppressed life. However, in the eyes of the people and the Pharisees, Jesus was the son of a carpenter from Nazareth. They held that Jesus was blaspheming by claiming He was the Son of God. Another possible reason was that the gospel was based on faith in Jesus, the Savior, not on good works or observing the Law, which was directly contrary to the Pharisees' teaching. These great offenses, fueled by his religious conviction and zeal, created in Saul a terrible hatred for Christ's followers and he persecuted the Christ-followers to death.

Saul believed strongly his belief and religion were *right* and the only possible way to righteousness. In addition to the lens of self-righteousness resulting from religious performance, Saul also had the lens of pride that tunneled his vision. The spirit of religion blinded him, causing him to separate and categorize people into different groups. Saul was on a mission to eliminate those people who, according to him, held wrong beliefs.

Wikipedia defines self-righteousness as "a feeling or display of . . . moral superiority derived from a sense that one's beliefs, actions, or affiliations are of greater virtue than those of the average person. Self-righteous individuals are often intolerant of the opinions and behaviors of others."

The Oxford (Lexico) dictionary definition of pride is "a feeling of deep pleasure or satisfaction derived from one's achievements." My experience and observations of pride are that it is often manifested as easily offended, judgmental, a separation of self from others based on beliefs, behavior, race, or culture.

Saul had three sets of tainted lenses:

- The lens of religion, which causes the viewer to categorize and label people, things, and beliefs to justify the superiority of their own opinion, action, and purpose.

- The lens of self-righteousness, which causes the viewer to think they always know what is wrong with other people. Their way is the only way and the best way of doing things.

- The lens of pride, which causes the viewer to look down on other people who are of a lower position, status, or standing, or those with fewer achievements.

Through one encounter with Jesus, everything changed.

"As he was traveling, it happened that he was approaching Damascus, and suddenly a light from heaven flashed around him; and he fell to the ground and heard a voice saying to him, 'Saul, Saul, why are you persecuting Me?' And he said, 'Who are You, Lord?' And He said, 'I am Jesus whom you are persecuting, but get up and enter the city, and it will be told you what you must do.' The men who traveled with him stood speechless, hearing the voice but seeing no one. Saul got up from the ground, and though his eyes were open, he could see nothing; and leading him by the hand, they brought him into Damascus. And he was three days without sight, and neither ate nor drank" (Acts 9:3–9).

People with the lenses of religion, pride, and self-righteousness cannot really see, even if their physical eyes are open. In Saul's eyes, the battle was about righteousness and evil. In God's eyes, the fight was against Him because He is the embodiment of righteousness.

The good news is Jesus provided a way for Saul to regain his sight. "So Ananias departed and entered the house, and after laying his hands on him said, 'Brother Saul, the Lord Jesus, who appeared to you on the road by which you were coming, has sent me so that you may regain your sight and be filled with the Holy Spirit.' And immediately there fell from his eyes something like scales, and he regained his sight, and he got up and was baptized" (Acts 9:17–18).

Thank God, Ananias heard God. It must have been a frightening thing to confront and lay hands on Saul, the most zealous killer of the believers in Jesus. But Ananias bravely obeyed God, and Saul regained his sight. Our healing and the transformation of our lenses are always in God's plan but their fulfillment depends on our obedience to God's voice, not least to His commandment for us to love one another as He has loved us first.

Saul experienced miraculous transformation as soon as the scales—the tainted lenses of religion, pride, and self-righteousness—fell off his eyes through the divine intervention of the laying on of hands and prayers of Ananias. His transformation is evident in his writings: "More than that, I count all things to be loss in view of the surpassing value of knowing Christ Jesus my Lord, for whom I have suffered the loss of all things, and count them but rubbish so that I may gain Christ, and may be found in Him, not having a righteousness of my own derived from the Law, but that which is through faith in Christ, the righteousness which comes from God on the basis of faith" (Philippians 3:8–9).

After the supernatural removal of the blinding scales, Saul received his heavenly vision (calling) as a minister and a witness to the Gospel as the Apostle Paul, "to open their [Jews' and Gentiles'] eyes so that they may turn from darkness to light and from the dominion of Satan to God, that they may receive forgiveness of sins and an inheritance among those who have been sanctified by faith in Me" (Acts 26:18).

Perhaps people who struggle to hear from God about their calling may benefit from removing the taints from their lenses that are probably locking their hearing and vision.

Questions to ponder:

+ *Do you have the lens of religion?*
+ *Do you have the lens of self-righteousness?*
+ *Do you have the lens of pride?*

LENS OF UNGODLY EXPECTATION

King David said, "My soul, wait thou only upon God; for my expectation is from him" (Psalm 62:5 KJV). Often, we look to other people to meet our needs when, in fact, God is the only one who can truly meet our needs and expectations. The tendency to look to others rather than to God is called *ungodly expectations.*

Ungodly expectations can strain our relationships because they fall short of what we want and need. A relationship issue with an authority figure in the workplace is often a reflection of a relationship issue with an authority figure in the family.

I grew up in an Asian family. My parents were trained by their parents to do more or do better by telling them what they have not done, or not done well. Rarely would we hear words of affirmation. We needed to do more and better so we could enter a superior school so we could get a well-paid job and have enough money for a good life.

In 2014, we moved as a family to Hong Kong for my husband's expat assignment and were resident there for three years. Our second daughter, who was three years old, started to attend kindergarten in a well-known Christian school. Her teacher refused to praise the children for a job well done. The school staff believed words of affirmation would make the children proud. Instead, they determined to train the children to be humble by withholding affirmation.

This culture propels and perpetuates the principle of "never good enough." We believe we are *good* by striving to get to the next level. Identifying the very next goal and trying our best to get there as fast as we can is a pattern of thinking that seems to work well for us. Look at where we are now—vice president of a company—not too shabby, so let's continue the journey. We get married and start to train our children to do and achieve more by reminding them of the "not good enough" principle. After all, we were raised that way and it worked out well for us. Until one day, our children don't respond or even rebel against our nagging about "not good enough."

Throughout my career, I had the privilege of working with many talented and caring leaders. My personal and professional growth under those leaders was exciting and rewarding. However, I did struggle with one particular kind of leader: very talented, super-intelligent, but critical. I admired and respected this particular leader's gifting and intelligence, but I felt ultimately defeated by the remarks of not measuring up and not being enough.

Gradually, I noticed a toxic pattern: I was striving to earn my leader's approval and affirmation. It took three crashes for me to realize the taint on my lenses when viewing myself: I am not enough, I am not worthy, and my value and worth are in what my leader says I am. My starting point was *lacking, not enough, not worthy*, and my desired endpoint was *abundance, valuable, worthy*. My life had been on a performance treadmill, moving from the starting point of *lack* and trying to arrive at the endpoint of *abundance*.

When we get into the striving mode, we often don't discern it. Signs are evident to those who are close to us: long working hours, back pain, shoulder pain, ignoring or even ceasing to be part of the family. Passion for greatness sometimes masks the drive to achieve. It is acceptable to sacrifice sleep, health, and family for the higher and more noble purpose—that is what we believe, even though family tension is rising. Until one day, the artificial world we are building out of our own self-effort crashes down. Often, our loved ones, who know us well, reveal our tainted lenses.

You may argue growth and increase are in our DNA. In the creation, God blessed man to multiply and take dominion. The desire to grow in every area of our lives is in our design. What is the difference between striving to achieve and growing as God commands? The difference is in the *starting point*. The basis for striving is a self-view of lack or not being enough. Growth as God intended is based on our view of *His* abundance and *His* limitless resources in us and for us; we merely partner with God to progressively manifest His abundant riches in us. He does all the heavy lifting, and we have a part to play in the process.

In the workplace, finding your strengths and weakness in the Myers-Briggs personality type indicator is very common. I remember my forte was always goal-oriented, results-oriented, or task-oriented. When we look in the mirror, we see the reflection of God as we believe Him to be. One day, as I asked the Holy Spirit to reveal the different lenses I might have, I suddenly realized I had a tainted lens in viewing God; I was viewing God as though He values tasks, results, and accomplishments more than He values me as a person.

I know where this lens came from: my father and my father's father. This is prevalent in the Chinese culture. I forgave my forefathers and I forgave my father; he inherited this belief and practiced it on me, and by doing so, he passed it on to me. I also renounced the lie that Father God was like my father—a taskmaster, valuing my accomplishments more than who I am.

Until I dealt with the tainted lens through which I saw God and forgave my father and my forefathers, I continued to run into authority figures who seemed to value my accomplishments more than who I am.

In her article entitled *Unhappy Employees Outnumber Happy Ones By Two To One Worldwide*, Susan Adams of Forbes cited a 2013 report claiming there are "87% of workers worldwide who, as Gallup puts it, 'are emotionally disconnected from their workplaces and less likely to be productive.' In other words, work is more often a source of frustration than one of fulfillment for nearly 90% of the world's workers." Meaning, "Gallup found that only 13% of workers feel engaged by their jobs."[2]

Work to the majority of workers is merely a means to earn a living. You can imagine the frustration an unhappy worker brings to home and family. Spouses, children, and loved ones become reluctant heroes with no choice but to share the pain and frustration.

Many people quit their day job and start their own independent business, hoping to find fulfillment from their dream job. But true satisfaction is an inside job. We can change what we *do*, but our dissatisfaction towards self, others, and God will eventually catch up and manifest itself in one way or another.

Jim Clifton, Chairman and CEO at Gallup, wrote in 2017, "According to Gallup's World Poll, many people in the world hate their job and especially their boss."[3] Interestingly, it's the unhappy, unfulfilled, and less engaged workers who hate their boss. "Hate" is a strong word, and it is a form of lens; it distorts how a person sees other people. It divides people.

Many times, people look to their boss as their identity affirmer, opportunity and promotion provider, and defender when conflict arises. Often, they are very disappointed and are left feeling their boss has let them down. Some leaders encourage their workers, provide when there is an opportunity, and defend and even take on responsibility when their team fails to deliver; but not every leader believes in or possesses this level of leadership caliber. Some leaders want their employees to fear them so their ego and sense of superiority can be satisfied.

Is it solely the leader's responsibility when a leader-employee relationship turns sour? Of course not. Very often, it is the employee's lenses that prevent them from seeing their leader as who they truly are. They project their expectations onto their leader when, in fact, those expectations should be fulfilled by God alone.

The Bible also instructs us, "Whatever you do, do your work heartily, as for the Lord rather than for men, knowing that from the Lord you will receive the reward of the inheritance. It is the Lord Christ whom you serve" (Colossians 3:23–24).

Consider the authority figures in your life. If you keep running into a leader or boss who values your accomplishments more than who you are, you might be seeing God through a tainted lens, and you might need to forgive the person who wrote those lies on your heart.

Questions to ponder:

+ *What is the motivation for doing your job (well)?*
+ *Are you striving, or are you partnering with God in your job?*

✦ *How is your relationship with your boss? Do you work hard to earn your leader's approval and affirmation?*

✦ *Do you see a pattern of leader-and-subordinate relationships in your career?*

LENS OF PAST

When we first moved to Hong Kong in 2014, I was eager and ready to apply everything I had learned in the United States to change Hong Kong. I believed my gifting and skills would benefit Hong Kong. To my surprise, the church community which we were attending there didn't even allow us to minister.

It was a difficult season as I struggled with who I was without being able to use my gifting to help people. I had a series of dreams over that period. All these dreams revealed the same message: do not rely on your past success and glory; follow God as He is doing a new thing.

We tend to rely on our past when our ways and methodologies have been effective and successful. After all, it worked then so surely, it's going to work again; why re-invent the wheel? The lenses of past stopped me from partnering with God in facing the unknown; they became a manner of self-reliance.

By God's mercy, He showed me the tainted lens of the past through dreams and I was able to repent for relying on my past successes. Replacing the lens of the past with the lens of faith resulted in more trust in God. Soon after, God opened a door for us to be with a family faith community, where each individual is a family member and has something to give and to receive. We felt right at home. In this new community, we served people with our gifting and skills, and we also received much from each of these spiritual family members. Looking back, it was one of the most fulfilling seasons of our lives in Hong Kong.

The 19th Century Danish philosopher and theologian, Søren Kierkegaard, once said, "Life can only be understood backwards; but it must be lived forwards."[4] Some people spend a large amount of their lifetime lamenting past failures. Others dwell on their previous success and continue to run their life according to what has worked before. Neither of these approaches help people to move forward in their lives. I have stood in both places before. The tainted lens of the past is the culprit that leads us to remain in stagnant waters where there is no longer life flowing in and out of us.

In Genesis 19, God sent angels to destroy Sodom, the city where Lot and his family resided. By the mercy of God and the intercession of Abraham, God spared Lot's family from the destruction. The angels' clear instructions to Lot included two commands to "escape" and two "do not's". "When they had brought them outside, one said, 'Escape for your life! Do not look behind you, and do not stay anywhere in the valley; escape to the mountains, or you will be swept away'" (Genesis 19:17). Unfortunately, not everyone heeded the angels' orders. "But his wife, from behind him, looked back, and she became a pillar of salt" (Genesis 19:26). One of the Bible translations says Lot's wife looked back longingly.

This passage is a warning to all humankind: leave the land of sin, past, and familiarity behind and do not look back. When you look back, it will resume its hold on you. You will never move forward to your future, where God's promise waits for you. In his book, *The Purpose Driven Life: What on Earth Am I Here For?* Pastor Rick Warren says, "We are products of our past, but we don't have to be prisoners of it."[5]

Is looking back to your past that bad? Will looking back to our history and to what is familiar going to turn us into a pillar of salt, a lifeless statue?

I have served in the Inner Healing ministries for the past ten years. It is a powerful ministry that helps to free people from the torment of past hurts and wounds, and replace lies with the truth about who they are and who God is. I've witnessed the dramatic transformation of hundreds of people's lives when past hurts and wounds lose their grip. They were then able to see God as a good Father and themselves as children of God.

I have learned that sometimes it's easier for people to be past-focused than to face the future with faith and hope. Humans tend to look backward as opposed to moving forwards. There is familiarity and certainty in the past. You know what you're going to get, whether it's good or bad; the future, on the other hand, is less certain.

Many people who dwell in the past for a long time cannot imagine what the future holds. Their lens of past blocks their vision and prevents them from seeing the joy of fulfilled promises by stepping into the unknown. The Word of God says, "Forget the former things; do not dwell on the past. See, I am doing a new thing! Now it springs up; do you not perceive it? I am making a way in the wilderness and streams in the wasteland" (Isaiah 43:18–19 NIV).

Dwelling on the past is the same as staying in a wasteland without hope. God loves us so much, and He is calling us to lift our head from the past and memories of former things so we can see and understand something new He is doing to get us out of our hopelessness.

Dwelling on the past causes us to miss out on the new things God is doing. The Apostle Paul, who wrote thirteen of the New Testament books, said this: "Brethren, I do not regard myself as having laid hold of it yet; but one thing I do: forgetting what lies behind and reaching forward to what lies ahead" (Philippians 3:13).

Instead of dwelling on our past failures and successes, God instructs us to remember His deeds and His wonders. "I shall remember the deeds of the Lord; surely I will remember Your wonders of old" (Psalm 77:11).

When we meditate on His miracles in our lives, we become hopeful. When we dwell on our past failures, we feel like a failure and start to agree with the thought of "I am a failure." I did that.

When we focus on our previous successes, we might make a formula out of it. His instruction is to guide us into His ways of thinking and living so we will walk in peace and have prosperous lives. We look for the deeds of the Lord and remember His wonders of old when we survey our past. Even in the depths of our past hurt, pain, and wounds, we can still find the good deeds of the Lord.

Elizbeth Smart was abducted by a rapist and kept in captivity for nine months until she was found. Anyone who went through what she had would most probably be a slave to their past and become hopeless. The advice from her mom changed Elizabeth's lens from the desperate past to a hopeful future: "Elizabeth, what this man has done is terrible. There aren't any words that are strong enough to describe how wicked and evil he is! He has taken nine months of your life that you will never get back again. But the best punishment you could ever give him is to be happy. To move forward with your life. To do exactly what you want. . . . You be happy, Elizabeth. Just be happy. If you go and feel sorry for yourself, or if you dwell on what has happened, if you hold on to your pain, that is allowing him to steal more of your life away."[6]

That was what she did. She declared that the abusers have no power over her. She threw away the lens of a victim based on her past and put on the lens of a victor for a bright future. She went on to finish her high school and college. She got married, had kids, and became an activist for American child safety, a journalist, and a harpist.

As a leader in a corporate organization, I used to conduct a lot of interviews to hire talented people for the company. One of the methods that worked really well in identifying whether or not the interviewee would be the right fit is to ask questions about their past failures and successes, and particularly how they handle failure. The assumption is if you've done something before, you are likely to do it again. The organization is looking for people with *successful* track records. Today's society is less likely to look at the person who has failed with a fresh perspective, and less likely to give them a second chance.

People who see themselves through the lens of the past are inclined to see others with the same lens. Dennis is a leader at a prominent research institute. He underwent an extended period of healing from his troubled upbringing and family. He tends to cut himself off from people by whom he feels threatened and wounded. He carries the rejection within him; it shows on his face and in his demeanor. He was not approved to serve as a ministry leader. This record of rejection prevented him from serving as a leader in other ministries. Even though through inner healing he has become more open, he still has a fear of rejection.

Dennis is an example of the two-way power of lenses. The lens of the past blocks people from seeing him as he is now, and it blocks him from seeing people as God sees them. Tainted lenses reinforce divisions between people and keep them from experiencing true freedom and love.

The lens of the past keeps us stuck in our history as well as other people's history, and is opposite of the love defined in the Bible. "Love is patient and kind. Love is not jealous or boastful or proud or rude. It does not demand its own way. It is not irritable, and it keeps no record of being wronged" (1 Corinthians 13:4–5 NLT).

The lens of love keeps no record of wrongs. It is like a mighty flooding wave, rushing over the barricades built from the lens of the past; it reconciles people, especially people with records of failure.

Questions to ponder:

+ *Is past failure on your mind most of the time?*
+ *What are the areas in your life within which you are still riding on past glory and success?*
+ *Is there anyone in your life you see through the lens of the past?*
+ *What are the wonders of God from the past you speak about and share with others?*

10

TAINTED LENSES—
A SOUL PERSPECTIVE

Revealing Responses

*Paradigms are like glasses. When you have incomplete
paradigms about yourself or life in general, it's like wearing
glasses with the wrong prescription. That lens affects
how you see everything else.*

—Sean Covey

We need glasses to correct our vision when the images
become blurry and we receive less than optimal
light into our lens. We have distorted spiritual
vision because our lenses have deviated from the original lens
of God. In other words, our filters have become tainted or our
paradigms have become flawed and incomplete.

We grow accustomed to our inner vision or lenses. They
become part of our being. How can we identify the taints
when they are so familiar to us? In the coming pages, I propose
how we may identify the taints in our heart, eyes, and mouth.

The book of Proverbs advises us: "Watch over your heart with all diligence, for from it flow the springs of life. Put away from you a deceitful mouth and put devious speech far from you. Let your eyes look directly ahead and let your gaze be fixed straight in front of you. Watch the path of your feet and all your ways will be established. Do not turn to the right nor to the left; turn your foot from evil" (Proverbs 4:23–27).

Now let's examine our heart, eyes, and mouth (speech) and how these may reveal our tainted lenses.

OUR HEART

Our heart condition reveals the taints of our lenses, and our lenses reflect our heart condition. I am not proposing to change the Word of God in the Bible but to paraphrase Proverbs 4:23, "Watch over your heart *[lens]* with all diligence, for from it flow the springs of life." The issue of life starts from the heart—our words, gaze or focus, and walk all reveal the condition of our heart and, similarly, our lenses.

In the Old Testament, King Saul kept David in his house after the young shepherd had killed Goliath with a stone from his sling. 1 Samuel 18:7 tells us, "The women sang as they played, and said, 'Saul has slain his thousands, and David his ten thousands.'" King Saul was overwhelmed with jealousy and insecurity. In reality, he had been rejected by God as king because of his own disobedience. Instead of looking within, he blamed David.

It is the envy (or jealousy) rising up from within that contaminates a person. Jesus explained this concept to his disciples. "For from within, out of the heart of men, proceed the evil thoughts, fornications, thefts, murders, adulteries, deeds of coveting and wickedness, as well as deceit, sensuality, envy, slander, pride and foolishness. All these evil things proceed from within and defile the man" (Mark 7:21–23).

And so it was with King Saul. "So from that time on Saul kept a jealous eye on David" (1 Samuel 18:9 NLT). When jealousy filled King Saul's heart, his lens became tainted.

In previous chapters, I have shared my journey toward recognizing the tainted lenses of idolatry, fear, hatred, pride, injustice, and ungodly expectation. These lenses all reflect heart conditions.

OUR EYES

Lack of focus may also reveal tainted lenses. It took me almost three months to finish three rounds of self-editing of this book, whereas it probably could have taken one month of focused effort to finish it. I often allow other things to hack my time. Until one day, I heard a saying: procrastination is a form of fear. While my gaze is on completion of the book, it is also on many other things. My walk shows procrastination and this symptom points to a taint on my lens: the fear of failure, or a fear of being seen.

In his article entitled *The Lamp of the Body Is the Eye*, Yves I-Bing Cheng talks about diplopia or double vision. "Instead of having our whole attention focused on God, we have one eye on God and another eye on the world. Your loyalty is divided between God and someone or something else. That is spiritual double vision."[1]

I feel this is a significant revelation regarding tainted lenses—the lens of double vision. Double vision, a divided heart, and double-mindedness all represent the same thing. The Apostle James emphasized the need to get rid of double-mindedness to be closer to God. "Draw near to God and He will draw near to you. Cleanse your hands, you sinners; and purify your hearts, you double-minded" (James 4:8).

OUR MOUTH

According to Apostle James, the smallest part of the body can cause the most problems.

"So also the tongue is a small part of the body, and yet it boasts of great things. See how great a forest is set aflame by such a small fire! And the tongue is a fire, the very world of iniquity; the tongue is set among our members as that which defiles the entire body, and sets on fire the course of our life, and is set on fire by hell" (James 3:5–6).

I served in the Healing Rooms and inner healing ministry where I have seen people receive tremendous breakthroughs and healing through prayer. Only weeks later, they come back with the same conditions because of their unbridled mouth. They start to speak out and agree with the negative symptoms they feel. It is almost like you get what you say.

Growing up in Asian culture, we are good at correcting and pointing out our children's faults. That was the way I was treated as a child, and I treated my children the same way. As Christians, we as parents ought to speak out the way God sees our children. And yet, it is such a struggle to speak out *you are a world changer* by faith when they resist our requests to do simple tasks such as the dishes. The outcome will continue to be *my children do not like to do chores* because I keep saying my children don't like to do chores.

I agree with the Apostle James: "But no one can tame the tongue; it is a restless evil and full of deadly poison. With it, we bless our Lord and Father, and with it we curse men, who have been made in the likeness of God; from the same mouth come both blessing and cursing. My brethren, these things ought not to be this way" (James 3:8–10). And, "Death and life are in the power of the tongue, and those who love it will eat its fruit" (Proverbs 18:21).

But there is hope for us to be free from the sins of the mouth. "If we confess our sins, He is faithful and righteous to forgive us our sins and to cleanse us from all unrighteousness" (1 John 1:9).

In the next few sections, we will examine different forms of negative responses from our mouth as a result of having tainted lenses. These include being judgmental, complaining, being critical, gossiping, slander, being triggered, offended, and bitter.

Being Judgmental

One day, we met an acquaintance at church. Her face was unusually red. "Are you OK?" I asked her. "Your face is red."

She shied away from me without answering. Little did I know this kind of greeting was taboo in the American culture. My husband and older daughter gave me a lecture on cultural inappropriateness. In America, you do not comment on looks or speak to a person about their appearance unless you have gained permission, they explained. I am still learning about cultural etiquette after living here for more than twenty years.

In the country where I grew up, we greet people with, "Have you eaten?" because having enough food to eat was the primary concern of people at that time. If we see someone who looks ill, we go and ask if that person is okay. Chinese people are more direct with their comments or judgments. An immigration officer in Shanghai once told my husband, "Hi, you have gained some weight and you look chubbier," while looking at his passport photo.

That morning in church, I was concerned for the wellbeing of our acquaintance, so I asked her what was wrong. However, my asking caused her embarrassment as the reason for her red face was the new blush she had used.

The strong reaction I received from this incident caused me to dig deeper into the cause and effects of judgment. Making judgments in our hearts or pronouncing judgment toward another person reveals our tainted lenses. I had assumed something was wrong with her face when I asked her about it. My question arose from my concern for her; nonetheless it was a judgment on her appearance.

The Greek word for judgment is *krima*, which means "condemnation of wrong, the decision (whether severe or mild) which one passes on the faults of others."[2] Jesus used this same word. "For with what judgment you judge, you will be judged; and with the measure you use, it will be measured back to you" (Matthew 7:2 NKJV). When we judge others, we will be judged. "But do you suppose this, O man, when you pass judgment on those who practice such things and do the same yourself, that you will escape the judgment of God?" (Romans 2:3). When we judge others and then do the same things as the person on whom we passed judgment, we are subject to the judgment of God.

When I explained this concept to my teenage daughter, she immediately understood it and said, "That means I judge myself when I judge others." Writer, speaker, and author, Earl Nightingale, once said, "When you judge others, you do not define them, you define yourself."

Everyone has a sense of right and wrong but a person's lenses will filter their sense of right and wrong. Therefore, the *right* that a person believes may not be the truth, but it is perceived as the truth by that person. It is a judgment when someone forms an opinion or evaluation of another person based on a perceived truth.

In a parent and child relationship, a child judges his parent based on his perceived truth. Often, this happens when parents fail to meet the child's needs or fail to keep a promise. For example, when a father is always busy with his work and absent from his child's life, the child may judge him for not being a good father when he sees his friend's father is present at all his life events.

In my years of Inner Healing ministry, I have often seen judgments blind or block people from seeing others for who they really are. The judgment also prevents those people from experiencing true forgiveness. People judge others as a way of self-preservation but it is false protection. And yet, it is such a familiar way of life to us we don't even discern we are operating in judgment.

People pass judgment all the time, such as in employer-employee relationships, leader-subordinate relationships, parent-children relationships. The President of the United States is judged by people around the world—it's there for all to see in social media.

The one who judges others has the same traits or characteristics as the one being judged. Most times, the judging person doesn't realize this, as Jesus pointed out with this illustration: "Why do you look at the speck that is in your brother's eye, but do not notice the log that is in your own eye? Or how can you say to your brother, 'Let me take the speck out of your eye,' and behold, the log is in your own eye? You hypocrite, first take the log out of your own eye, and then you will see clearly to take the speck out of your brother's eye" (Matthew 7:3–5).

I love this parable—it amplifies the effect so we can grasp the difference in tainted lenses between the judge and the one being judged. A speck is very much smaller than a log. A log will completely block your vision, while a speck will make your eye uncomfortable and irritated. Imagine this picture: while your view is blocked by a log big enough to cover your face, you point your finger at another person who has a speck of dust in his eye, saying, "Take that spot of dust out of your eyes so you can see better."

Ashley sat in front me, fuming about her mother. "How could she marry this guy who had violated me and never treats me with respect and honor? I've suffered so much because of her decision to marry this guy." She had probably forgiven her mom seventy times seven over the years but she was still harboring hatred for her mom.

"Is there anything else you would like to forgive your mom about?" I asked.

Silence.

"I forgive her for marrying the wrong guy; I forgive her for putting religion before us, her children; I forgive her for saying I am not enough; I forgive her for comparing me with my siblings."

Ashley experienced some relief from the words of forgiveness she spoke, but I sensed she was still feeling some irritation toward her mom.

"Did you ever make an inner vow, for example, 'I never want to be like my mom when I grow up?'" I asked.

"Oh, yeah, how did you know?" Ashley suddenly had a revelation as I led her toward renouncing the judgment of her mom and breaking off her inner vows. "I only see her inadequacies and mistakes," she said. "Wow, I've been so busy judging my mom that I wasn't aware I've been doing that."

"Could you put on Jesus' lenses of love, look at your mom, and describe what you see?"

Ashley thought about this for a bit and then said, "My mom was hurt and afraid. She's also kindhearted, and I have compassion for her."

The lights had gone on, exposing the taints on her lenses. After Ashley removed the lens of judgment, she was able to see her mom as God sees her: hurt, afraid, kindhearted, and with compassion. Her resentment and unforgiveness evaporated, enabling her to have a much better relationship with her mom since then.

Replacing tainted lenses with the lens of love is powerful.

Questions to ponder:

+ *Do you have a habit of judging others? How is that working out for you?*

+ *What happened to a relationship when you suspended judgement and replaced it with the lens of love?*

TAINTED LENSES—A SOUL PERSPECTIVE

Complaining

Author Jessica Jones in her book, *Love What You Have: A Real Truth about Why You Always Complain or How to Get Maximum from Your Life Today* says, "Negativity and complaining are like a virus. It only takes a little bit of exposure before you are completely overtaken. Then, the more you feed it, the better the climate for the virus, and the worse your attitude becomes."[3]

I must confess I was a master complainer. I didn't recognize this trait in me until I saw the fruit of it. I complained about complainers (in my view they are complainers) for a very long time. When I complained about the complainers, it was in the hope of changing them; instead, it led both sides downhill into blaming and drained energy. Complaining about complainers was exhausting. The feelings of aggression and the grumbling voice become louder and louder, fostering bitterness, resentment, and even rejection.

Complaining creates a negative reality the complainer doesn't want. I later realized those whom I was complaining about and I were operating in the same spirit. After one fierce battle of complaining, it dawned on me this was not working. If I wanted different results, I would need to change my attitude and my action towards the person I was complaining about.

This revelation opened my eyes, enabling me to do something completely different. I made a list of the issues about which I'd been complaining, together with the expected responsibility and measurable outcomes. When the other complainer reviewed the written document, he started to take responsibility and action. I never dreamed putting words into writing could be so effective in resolving this conflict.

In God's eyes, when we complain about a person we are complaining against God as that person is made in the image of God. Their roles in our lives are not accidental but with purpose. The Bible teaches us about the consequences of

83

complaining. It will destroy a person: "Nor grumble, as some of them did, and were destroyed by the destroyer" (1 Corinthians 10:10). And it will bring judgment: "Do not grumble against one another, brothers, so that you may not be judged; behold, the Judge is standing at the door" (James 5:9 ESV).

In his blog entitled *The Root of a Complaining Spirit is . . .*, life coach, speaker, and author, Dean Trune, wrote, "I believe that the root issue for both inadequacy and complaining is self-centeredness. . . . I think that our bent towards having a complaining spirit is based on a misconception that the rest of creation exists to make me happy. . . . My attitude of self-centeredness will lead me to respond to life with a complaining spirit."[4]

The tainted lens of a complainer is self-idolatry as all they *see* makes them unhappy. They lose sight of what God is doing in their lives and other people's lives, as they have lost sight of His goodness.

Another tainted lens common to complainers is the lens of pride. Author and speaker John Bevere's article in Charisma Magazine, *How Complaining Halts Your Destiny*, puts it this way: "Complaining indirectly communicates to the Lord, 'I don't like what You are doing in my life—and if I were You, I would do it differently.' Complaining is nothing more than a manifestation of insubordination to God's authority. . . . Joseph feared God, and he never complained."[5]

According to Strong's Concordance, the Hebrew translation for a grumble or complaint (as in Exodus 15:24) is *tluwnah*, and the definition of *tluwnah* is *exalted* and *lofty*. Therefore, the Hebrew meaning of grumbling or complaining is to exalt oneself above others. The spirit behind complaining is pride and loftiness.

Grumbling was first mentioned in Exodus 15:24. "So the people grumbled at Moses, saying, 'What shall we drink?'" This happened after the people of Israel were delivered from Egypt and Pharaoh's slavery, and right after they sang a song to exalt the Lord for His marvelous salvation. They grumbled against Moses because they promoted their physical need over and above God's power of provision. They were thirsty and hungry; their need was so great they thought even God couldn't meet it. It's as if a giant mountain of unbelief blocked their vision of seeing God as their provider.

One reason for complaining is when we forget what God has done in our lives. That was the case in the story of the people of Israel who forgot God had mightily and miraculously parted the Red Sea and led them out of Egypt.

There is an Indian Proverb that says, "I had no shoes and complained until I met a man who had no feet."

We live in a society where some parents or caretakers relinquish their responsibilities and abandon their children to pursue their own way of living, or they expose their children to harm and hurt. Complaining against their parents and caretakers will not change these children's futures.

Since 2013, we have been to Cambodia several times for short-term mission trips. There, we've met some amazing young men and women who grew up in New Hope Orphanages sponsored by the South East Asian Prayer Center (SEAPC). Each of these young people have their own story of abandonment and broken hearts.

In the New Hope Orphanages, they come to know Jesus and learn to apply His words to their lives. They go to school to equip themselves and become doctors, engineers, and lawyers. They become powerful forces for transformation in Cambodia because they have Jesus in their heart, their lives, and their workplace. There is no hint of complaining in their speech, but only joy and hope for a great future.

We sponsor two boys who were abandoned by their parents. We visited them in Cambodia in 2019, and they were thankful, carefree, and looking forward to a bright future. Sok San wants to become a policeman, and Saveth desires to become a doctor. They no longer identify themselves as orphans but children of Almighty God. If an orphan doesn't complain, why should we?

Sherri Langton shared in her article, *The Danger of Complaining*, how to put complaining to death. "I revisit Gethsemane when irritations arise, yielding to God all I dogmatically hold dear. The more I do this, the more I regard complaining not as a right but as a weight I must strip off in order to reach the finish line (Hebrews 12:1)."[6]

Questions to ponder:

+ *Who or what do you complain about the most?*
+ *How often do you complain?*
+ *What are the tainted lenses that have led you into the habit of complaining?*
+ *What goodness of God in your life have you lost sight of because of complaining?*

Being Critical

In 2015, during our time in Hong Kong, I had the privilege of working with some ladies in the area of dream interpretation. If interpreted correctly, dreams can guide our lives. They are night parables, telling stories through symbolism. Some people are gifted in biblical dream interpretation, while others may develop this skill through understanding the parables in the Bible and with a lot of practice.

I took a class on biblical dream interpretation but I couldn't interpret dreams at all. I had always had dreams and later on learned it was one of the languages God uses to speak to me. As I practiced and learned to hear God through interpreted dreams, I noticed a trend: most dreams are corrective dreams, intended to reveal our blind spots and indicate we need to make corrections in our heart, words, or actions.

The majority of my dreams were corrective. I mentioned to one of my pastor friends that I dream almost every night. He said, "Oh, are you kind of stubborn?" That was not what I wanted to hear. And then I read a passage in the book of Job and understood what my friend was referring to. One of the purposes of night dreams is to keep man walking on the right path, to provide him with corrective guidance. "In a dream, a vision of the night, when sound sleep falls on men, while they slumber in their beds, then He opens the ears of men, and seals their instruction, that He may turn man aside from his conduct, and keep man from pride; He keeps back his soul from the pit, and his life from passing over into Sheol" (Job 33:15–18).

One morning, I woke up rather discouraged after another corrective dream. What, *again*? Why is God only interested in pointing out my blind spots? I asked God about it and what I heard was I had been deceived. This led me to search the Bible about dreams that deceive and I found it says we should be wary of dreams that are not sent from God. "For thus says the Lord of hosts, the God of Israel: Do not let your prophets and your diviners who are in your midst deceive you, nor listen to your dreams which you cause to be dreamed. For they prophesy falsely to you in My name; I have not sent them, says the Lord" (Jeremiah 29:8–9 NKJV).

The tainted lenses of our heart can induce our dreams, with our beliefs and the lenses through which we view God, ourselves, and others conditioning the dreams we receive. If my view of God is that He is only interested in pointing out nothing but my shortcomings, weaknesses, and sins (despite this view being inconsistent with who God is in the Bible), then I will most probably keep receiving dreams about God pointing out my sins.

This seems to demonstrate a conflict between our conscious and subconscious minds. We may consciously know something based on facts or even experience, but our subconscious mind has not caught up with it—it still sees through the tainted lens that God is critical. Our image of Father God may be skewed by our experiences of our own family or leaders but this view of God is inconsistent with His character as it is reflected in the Bible. When this is the case, we need to replace our tainted lenses with the lens of love, so we can see God as He really is.

My dreams have shifted after I renounced the lie that God is only interested in pointing out my weaknesses. For example, in one of my dreams, President Trump and the First Lady were dancing; he swung back, turned his head toward me and said, "Wei Wei, your English is very good." I said to him, "No, my English is bad; I speak *Chinglish* (Chinese English)." The dream revealed my insecurity about my words and criticality of myself. In this dream, President Trump represents God. The good news is God Himself affirmed me. Instead of disagreeing with what He said about me, I should agree with Him. This dream revealed to me that God was pleased with what I say.

The person who views others as being critical is very often the most critical of him/herself. Inspirational author, Shannon L. Alder, writes, "Often those that criticize others reveal what he himself lacks."[7] It could be due to a generational trait, or a deeply rooted rejection. The good news is that once we recognize it, we can bring it to the cross. There is no sin so great His cross and blood cannot redeem.

Questions to ponder:

+ *Do you see God as being critical of you?*
+ *Through what lenses do you view God?*
+ *Are you critical of yourself?*
+ *What tainted lenses do you have when viewing yourself?*

TAINTED LENSES—A SOUL PERSPECTIVE

Gossiping

Gossip affects our relationship with others. The Greek philosopher Socrates once said, "Strong minds discuss ideas, average minds discuss events, weak minds discuss people."[8]

There is a parable story about gathering feathers that illustrates the damage gossip can cause.[9] To paraphrase it, one day, a woman repeated a nasty piece of gossip about a friend. The news traveled and soon everyone knew the ugly story. The lies set about and betrayal by a friend deeply hurt the subject of the gossip.

The woman who started the gossip was wracked with guilt over the pain she'd caused her friend. She approached a wise man for advice. He told her to buy a chicken, kill it, and drop its feathers along the road. She did what the wise man told her to. The next day, he told her to go and collect all the feathers she had dropped the day before. She was astonished; "It's not possible," she cried, "as all the feathers have blown away."

The wise man's intent was to illustrate the effect of gossip: it doesn't take much to spread it but once it's out there, you can never undo the hurt. You can only ask for forgiveness.

Gossip goes hand-in-hand with complaining. My definition of gossip is talking about someone else, especially about a person's shortcomings, weaknesses, and faults. Examining the instances when I've heard gossip or entered into a conversation during which someone has revealed another person's secrets, I've concluded the heart motivation behind gossip may be:

- To show and prove to others we are right and they are wrong.

- To show superiority; talking about other people's problems and weaknesses makes us feel good about ourselves.

- To seek revenge from unresolved bitterness, envy, jealousy, and hatred by hanging out other people's dirty laundry.

89

- To seek agreement and alliance.

- To create division.

- To vent frustration.

- To gain attention.

It is clear the motivation for gossip is not love; rather, it is the opposite of love. The gossiping person's tainted lenses would be hatred, pride, murder, and self-righteousness.

Gossip damages our lives. I received my daughter's permission to share this event. My daughter experienced tremendous pain due to a gossip incident during her last year of high school. One day, while having lunch, her friend said, "This guy you're tutoring, Mark, is weird and creepy." My daughter half-heartedly replied, "Yes, he is."

The next day, my daughter was called into the vice principal's office. "We got a report saying you slandered Mark and told people that he was weird and creepy," the vice principal said. "He's said you are not fit to be a tutor for him or anybody else."

My daughter came home in tears. How could a casual chat with her friend at the lunch table cause her to lose her good reputation and for all the good things she did to be forgotten? My daughter took responsibility for her part in the gossip; she humbled herself and apologized to Mark in the vice principal's office. She continued to help other students as a tutor after this incident.

Gossip is so rife people become desensitized to and ignorant of the damage it causes a person and a community. A gossip tale usually starts like this: "This is between you and me; please keep it confidential." To make it worse, confidential information often gets passed around with additions and subtractions based on the talebearer's personal opinions, causing what starts as one thing to end up as something completely different.

Martha's story is a good illustration of this phenomenon. Martha likes to talk about other people and make comments on their shortcomings although she doesn't intend to hurt anyone. One day over a coffee, Martha tells Brenda, her good friend from church, that the sermon from the associate pastor was not her favorite. It lacked content and depth, and it was boring. Brenda then tells her Bible study partner, Sandra, that there is a difference between someone who has a master's degree in divinity versus someone with only a bible college degree, as the sermon from the previous week demonstrated. She added she'd heard the same opinion from Martha.

Little did Brenda know but Sandra was a good friend of the associate pastor's wife. Sandra didn't dare repeat what she had heard directly to the associate pastor and his wife. So, she told the pastor's mom that people at church do not like his preaching. A few months later, the associate pastor resigned, hurt by all the gossip. It would have been better if Martha had provided direct feedback to the associate pastor himself; or, for anyone else who heard the gossip to nip it in the bud, by confronting their sin and putting a stop to it.

Often, for fear of confrontation, people spread what they have heard behind the back of the person being talked about. The consequence is character assassination and hurt for the subject of the gossip, as well as for all those who participated in and heard the gossip. As in this example described above, churches often split because they do not deal correctly with this sin. Indeed, "Death and life are in the power of the tongue, and those who love it will eat its fruit" (Proverbs18:21).

Gossip divides people. It causes misunderstanding even if, somehow, the person means well. Often, gossip robs a person of the opportunity to defend themselves. They may have changed in the meantime, with the gossip based on the previous version of themselves.

The Apostle Paul points out that gossip is one of the results of not acknowledging God for who He is. "And just as they did not see fit to acknowledge God any longer, God gave them over to a depraved mind, to do those things which are not proper, being filled with all unrighteousness, wickedness, greed, evil; full of envy, murder, strife, deceit, malice; they are gossips, slanderers, haters of God, insolent, arrogant, boastful, inventors of evil, disobedient to parents" (Romans 1:28–30).

Therefore, how we see God affects how we see others. When we see and acknowledge God for who He is, we will see others as God sees them.

Questions to ponder:

+ *Do you gossip?*
+ *When was the last time you gossiped?*
+ *Has gossip hurt you, or have you hurt anyone else with gossip?*

Slander

The Oxford Dictionary defines slander as "the action or crime of making a false spoken statement damaging to a person's reputation." In Psalm 101:5, the Lord warns, "Whoever secretly slanders his neighbor, him I will destroy."

We usually think people are slandered; in fact, a land can also be slandered. In the story of the people of Israel, Moses sent out twelve men from the twelve tribes to spy out the land Canaan. Ten men returned with a bad report of the land. "And the men, which Moses sent to search the land, who returned, and made all the congregation to murmur against him, by bringing up a slander upon the land" (Numbers 14:36 KJV). They gave an evil report, saying, "The land, through which we have gone to search it, is a land that eateth up the inhabitants thereof; and all the people that we saw in it are men of a great stature" (Numbers 13:32 KJV).

On the contrary, Joshua and Caleb gave a very positive report. "The land, which we passed through to search it, is an exceeding good land. If the Lord delight in us, then he will bring us into this land, and give it us; a land which floweth with milk and honey. Only rebel not ye against the Lord, neither fear ye the people of the land; for they are bread for us: their defence is departed from them, and the Lord is with us: fear them not" (Numbers 14:7–9 KJV).

Slandering reflects the lens of how we see God, self, and others. Joshua and Caleb's lenses through which they saw the land of Canaan were aligned with God's lens: yes, there are giants, but God is greater and He will disarm the giants and lead us to possess the land. They saw with a lens of faith. On the contrary, the bad report from the other ten men is based on their lenses of fear, or merely by their sight.

I often wonder what kind of report I would bring back if the Lord asked me to survey the land of Canaan? Would be it be by sight or by faith? Would I see through the lens of God or the lens of man? I would be slandering the land if my report was based merely on what I saw with my physical eyes.

Slanderous people tend to keep company with other slanderous people. In this way, their false reports can be continually circulated to a greater number of people and create even more divisions. One of the criteria for a church leader is not to be or not to have a wife who is slanderous (1 Timothy 3:11). Some church splits could be avoided if God's people didn't partner with those of a slandering spirit.

Questions to ponder:

+ *Has slander hurt you, or have you hurt anyone else with slander?*

+ *What lenses do you have that need to be replaced with the lens of love?*

Being Triggered

We all have triggers. A word or even a look can trigger a person to anger. Sometimes, a husband can be triggered by his wife's words because they remind him of his own critical parents' disapproval of him. American Coach Marshall Goldsmith defined triggers as "Our inner beliefs trigger failure before it happens. They sabotage lasting change by cancelling its possibility. We employ these beliefs as articles of faith to justify our inaction and then wish away the result. I call them belief triggers . . ."[10]

In 2017, we relocated from Hong Kong back to Arizona. We needed to find a house in a short period of time. My husband worked diligently to search the internet for a suitable home, sometimes discussing the various options on calls with our realtor. I felt I wasn't in the decision process. Strangely, during that time, all I wanted to do was be alone and go to sleep.

I went for an inner healing session and discovered the ordeal of searching for a house had triggered me. According to an article by the U. of Alberta published on Psych Central, "A *trigger* is something that sets off a memory tape or flashback transporting the person back to the event of her/his original trauma."[11] When I was young, my family made a decision about me without hearing my voice. During that past circumstance with my family, I protected myself with apathy and sleep. Hence, my coping mechanism became to go to sleep whenever I feel I don't have a voice.

The end of this particular story is I encountered Jesus and renounced the lie I didn't have a voice. I forgave the adults in my life who decided things without my voice, and I replaced the tainted lenses of the victim and voiceless with the lens of love. God Himself sings over me and dances around me. He is Father to the fatherless and gives a voice to the voiceless. I have not been triggered since then.

Our memory and senses can activate triggers. A trigger reveals tainted lenses, which many times have been caused by past trauma. The soul of a person—rather than their spirit—dominates the person when triggered. Triggers are a reaction to an unhealed heart, causing the person to operate out of will, emotions, and defense mechanisms.

Throughout the Bible, you can see Jesus was never triggered, regardless of the treatment He received. One person who was triggered a lot was King Saul. He was triggered to anger when women sang their praises of David's victory, saying it was more excellent than his. He was triggered to fear (of losing his kingdom to David) when he saw that David behaved wisely in all his ways and the Lord was with him.

Triggers can be illustrated by the story of a family friend, Charlie. When Charlie was born in Northern China in the 1950s, his mother was unwell. His family was poor and didn't have very much. Terrible sores infected his mother's nipples, preventing her from nursing Charlie. As he couldn't suck milk from her, he wasn't getting sufficient nutrients and his parents feared he might not survive. They took him to see a well-known folk doctor who, somehow, saved his life. His mom fed him rice porridge.

Charlie grew up throwing tantrums to get whatever he wanted. His dad either caved in or returned his outbursts with his fists, slapping him as he cursed him. Violence, dominance, control, manipulation, and wrath became Charlie's protection and way of life. Whenever he felt someone or something threatened his survival, he would erupt in rage and curse whoever stood in the way of getting what he wanted.

When Charlie is triggered, his family runs away. His wife, having gone through many ups and downs, fell into depression. With the grace of God, she learned to climb into the shadow of the Almighty God.

One day, Charlie—now in his 60s—had an argument with his wife. He felt he had been wronged and unjustly accused.

Angry, he left the house. His wife retreated to her prayer closet and poured her heart out to the Lord. About twenty minutes later, her phone rang; a policeman was on the line.

"Hi, is Charlie related to you?"

"Yes," Linda said, "he is my husband."

"I'm sorry to inform you that your husband has been in an accident. The good news is he didn't get hurt. He was riding his bicycle in the opposite direction of the traffic, and a car gently made contact with him before the driver braked. Would you be able to come and pick him up?"

"I'll come right away."

Charlie was shaken up. He seemed ashamed when his wife arrived, unable to look her in the eye. For the next few days, he pondered on all that had happened. He realized he saw God with the tainted lens of injustice, thinking, "God does not care about me and so I must take justice into my own hands." He could have been seriously hurt when the car hit him but instead, he escaped unscathed. He realized God protected him and was gracious to him. In fact, the police didn't cite him, even though he had been riding his bike in the wrong direction.

Charlie replaced his tainted lens with the lens of love—God is just and he would wait for His justice, letting God be *God* in his life. This change of lens was huge for Charlie and his family. The fear of God was restored in Charlie's life and his reactions are now mild and controlled when things don't go his way.

There is a deep root for each trigger. If you don't know your triggers, you can ask your spouse and your family, close friends, your coach, mentor, or pastors, and they will tell you. When you are triggered, it is a perfect time to engage with God. He loves for His children to come to Him, and He will reveal the tainted lenses preventing you from seeing God, self, and others as they ought to be.

Questions to ponder:

+ *Are you easily triggered?*
+ *What are your top three triggers?*
+ *What are the tainted lenses each trigger reveals?*

Being Offended

There was a time when my husband and I desperately wanted to have more children; even our seven-year-old daughter kept asking for a sibling. We prayed for a year and nothing happened. We prayed for another year and nothing happened. Our daughter, eight years old at the time, prayed for a little sister or brother every day but nothing happened.

One day, a man of God came into town and we lined up to receive his prayer for another child. Instead of praying, this man of God said to me, "Have you ever wanted to die? You need to seek experienced inner healing."

I was deeply offended by what he said. *Are you not a man of God?* I ranted in my mind. *We asked for a prayer of blessing for a breakthrough. You didn't do that; instead, you sent me away. Yes, I wanted to die when I was nineteen years old but I repented and moved on with my life.*

The offense simmered and my anger arose. Do you see the taints on my lens? I wanted the prayer *my* way and I wanted the blessing in *my* way. I got so upset when it came at me in a different way. The American writer, Mark Twain, said, "When people do not respect us we are sharply offended; yet deep down in his private heart no man much respects himself."[12] One of the definitions of *offense* given in the Oxford Dictionary is "annoyance or resentment brought about by a perceived insult to or disregard for oneself or one's standards or principles." A person who is easily offended will likely have a lens of pride or the lens of *my* ways (as opposed to God's ways).

THE LENS OF LOVE

The Pharisees were easily offended by Jesus—by whom He claimed to be, by what He said, and by what He did. On the contrary, Jesus was not easily offended. Instead, He said, "Blessed is he who is not offended because of Me" (Matthew 11:6 NKJV).

I finally recognized I was looking at our situation through the lens of *my* ways or pride. I have been tripped up by these lenses over and over again. I learned to surrender *my* ways for *His* ways and to recognize *His* ways are not *my* ways; *His* ways are higher. Surrendering enables the lens of *my* ways to be replaced by *His* ways.

I started my journey of inner healing with my family after picking up the lens of His ways. About one year into my inner healing journey, we discovered I was pregnant. What a wonderful surprise! Even my naturopathic doctor was surprised to hear this great news. To her, it was a miracle as she knew it would be difficult for me to conceive.

From my experience, what matters most is how we process the perceived offense. We have the choice of embracing it—letting it stick with us, soaking and fermenting into resentment and bitterness—or asking God to reveal our tainted lenses so we can release the offense and keep our walk free from any obstacles.

The Evangelist Luke wrote, "This being so, I myself always strive to have a conscience without offense toward God and men" (Acts 24:16 NKJV).

Questions to ponder:

- ✦ *When was the last time you took offense?*
- ✦ *How often do you get offended?*
- ✦ *Do you recognize the tainted lenses that cause you to be offended?*
- ✦ *What does it feel like when you exchange those lenses for the lens of love?*

Bitterness

The Cambridge Dictionary explains the adjective, *bitter*, in the following ways:[13]

- "Someone who is bitter is angry and unhappy because they cannot forget bad things that happened in the past"
- "A bitter experience causes deep pain or anger"
- "Expressing a lot of hate and anger"

For a huge part of my life, I was bitter about my lack of childhood. Consequently, I lived in the past for a very long time. God often speaks to me through dreams. As I wrote this section about bitterness, I had a dream. In my dream, a woman I know called Meryem came to visit me. I fed her bread, meat, and some spicy pickles. She ate all of these. Then she said, "I am looking for work; you're about to finish your book, so I can edit it and get paid." I told her I already have a publisher and pool of editors for my book so I don't need her services.

I pondered on the meaning and message of the dream. The exciting part was that the spiritual significance of *Meryem* is *bitterness*. The dream was to warn me not to feed the bitterness so as not to let it change my *book of life*.

In a Los Angeles Times article from May 25, 2009, Shari Roan reported that bitterness was the subject of a meeting of the American Psychiatric Association in San Francisco.[14] "You know them. I know them. And, increasingly, psychiatrists know them," Roan wrote. "People who feel they have been wronged by someone and are so bitter they can barely function other than to ruminate about their circumstances. This behavior is so common—and so deeply destructive—that some psychiatrists are urging it to be identified as a mental illness."

Roan goes on to quote German Professor and psychiatrist, Michael Linden, who believes bitterness is a very serious issue. The first to propose bitterness should be defined as a psychological disorder, he dubbed it "post-traumatic embitterment disorder," or PTED. Roan reports, "Embittered people are typically good people who have worked hard at something important, such as a job, relationship or activity, Linden says. When something unexpectedly awful happens—they don't get the promotion, their spouse files for divorce or they fail to make the Olympic team—a profound sense of injustice overtakes them." According to Linden, an estimated 1%–2% of population is embittered.

In the Harley Therapy Counselling Blog posted on May 12, 2015, entitled, *Bitterness—Why It Is a Real Psychological Concern*,[15] Sheri Jacobson states the long-term effects of bitterness include:

- Changes to a person's personality and self-image: "Dwelling on what happened allows bitterness to become a permanent part of your character, leaving your self-image to slide from competent and purpose-driven person to that of helpless victim."

- Elevation of cynicism and paranoia: "Bitterness can make you so self-protective you view the entire world through a jaundiced eye, avoiding opportunities and relationships that could be fulfilling."

- Stopping the clock of your life: "Dwelling on what hurt you keeps you trapped in the past, prolonging your pain and preventing you from moving forward with your life. It also stops you from being in the present moment, blinding you to any good things going on right in front of you."

- Wasted time and energy: "People who are bitter usually spend a fair amount of time replaying the event, retelling the event, and spinning out 'if only that hadn't happened' scenarios. And this takes time and energy, resources far more important than whatever was taken from you."

- Affected relationships: ". . . when someone obsessively complains or rehashes the same event again and again, eventually, it becomes draining on others. Bitterness can drive people you care about away while attracting other bitter people into your life."

To my surprise, when I reviewed these lists of the effects of bitterness, I could see traces of bitterness in my own life. The good news is I have fewer and fewer of these compared to five years ago.

Bitterness is often referred to as *wormwood* or *gall* in the Bible. Idolatry is like a bitterness-bearing root, as can be seen in this passage when the people of Israel were warned against turning away from their God, Yahweh, to serve the gods of other nations. ". . . so that there may not be among you man or woman or family or tribe, whose heart turns away today from the Lord our God, to go and serve the gods of these nations, and that there may not be among you a root bearing bitterness or wormwood" (Deuteronomy 29:18 NKJV).

In the book of Jeremiah, we see that because God's people had disobeyed His voice and did not walk in His ways, they would eat and drink bitterness. "The Lord said, 'Because they have forsaken My law which I set before them, and have not obeyed My voice nor walked according to it, but have walked after the stubbornness of their heart and after the Baals, as their fathers taught them,' therefore thus says the Lord of hosts, the God of Israel, 'behold, I will feed them, this people, with wormwood and give them poisoned water to drink" (Jeremiah 9:13–15). Lucifer was bitter towards God and so he led the rebellion against God with a third of the angels. Bitterness led him to kill, steal, and destroy God's creation of humankind. Like Lucifer, a bitter person has the lenses of pride and self-idolatry. The very first murder in the Bible was the story of Cain and Abel. Cain became consumed by bitterness as God was more pleased with his brother's offering and not so much with his. He felt he was unjustly treated and killed his brother. Bitterness kills.

A bitter person may kill others, but the bitterness will destroy a person from within. Elizabeth Cohen, Senior Medical Correspondent for CNN, documented a true story in August, 2011, entitled *Blaming others can ruin your health*.[16] "Kevin Benton had every reason to feel bitter," writes Cohen, going on to relate how he had been harassed and bullied nineteen years previously because he was an African-American in his sophomore year in college. "'I felt like I was being bullied, being targeted . . . I knew I couldn't retaliate in any way, or I'd lose my basketball scholarship.'"

Benton's first encounter with racism had a profound effect on him, starting with insomnia and then panic attacks. "Admitted to the hospital, he was found to have hypertrophic cardiomyopathy, or thickening of the muscles in the heart. The disease is the leading cause of heart-related sudden death in people under 30. So sick he couldn't walk, Benton lay in his hospital bed bitter and resentful. 'I thought to myself, "I've never hurt anybody. I serve in the community. I work with youth. I wrestled with God—why did this happen to me?"' he remembers. Just then, a janitor walked by and grabbed Benton's hand, and prayed aloud to God to heal him."

At the close of her prayer, he felt the physical changes in his body. "Benton forgave the students who had tormented them, and three days later, he walked out of the hospital. 'If I hadn't forgiven them, I'd be dead,' says Benton, now healthy and a social worker for the Philadelphia Department of Human Services."

According to neuroscience, bitterness and resentment do much damage to a human's brain. Author Lynn Hare considered Dr Caroline Leaf's book, *The Gift in You*, in her article on forgiveness.[17] Hare writes, "She says that there is a neurochemistry attached to thought clusters which throws our bodies into a chemical frenzy when we plant toxic seeds and grow them. When we don't forgive and when we hang onto pain and events, we are growing those toxic seeds."

Quoting Dr Leaf, Hare continues, "'Sometimes, it is so difficult to let go of those unbelievable and unjust things that happened to you. We feel that if we don't nurse them they won't get better, but that in itself is a lie from the enemy because they do get worse the more attention we pay to them.'"

We have a choice to continue to grow the tree of knowledge of good and evil (I am good, those who wronged me are evil), and nurse the root of bitterness to deeper ends through many future generations; or, we can uproot the tree of bitterness by repentance. I chose repentance and allowed the blood of Jesus to wash me clean. The peace in my mind only came after my repentance from bitterness.

Michelle struggled to see Audrey, her teenage daughter, with the lens of love. All she could see were her faults, her weaknesses, and shortcomings. Audrey didn't want to help out around the house with any chores. She challenged the rules set by her parents, from refusal to dump the trash nightly to demanding curfew time be later than 10:00 pm. Michelle would enforce the rules by grounding her; Audrey would rebel with reasons, excuses, and relentless arguing. Any conversation between them would start well but soon sparked into fire and they would both end up burned. Michelle would say sorry, Audrey would sometimes apologize after her father's peacemaking efforts, and so on, around and around in circles.

Michelle knew she had allowed bitterness to take root in her heart. Audrey often confronted Michelle with spicy, bitter words. One day, during a conversation about a struggle she'd had with Audrey, Michelle was reminded of the law of sowing and reaping. She realized she had sown bitterness and she was harvesting abundant bitter fruit from her daughter. A harvest is a multiplication of the seed. The only way to get rid of the plentiful harvest of bitterness in Audrey towards

Michelle would be to get rid of the seed. And it needed to start with Michelle.

Michelle and her daughter both had lenses of pride and self-idolatry, which was why they butted heads all the time—neither one of them was willing to humble themselves. The Holy Spirit convicted Michelle; she was ready to humble herself. She repented of the bitterness in her heart and humbly climbed off her high horse of being the mother and authority figure. Her relationship with her daughter immediately started to change for the better.

We often forget we are commanded by God to rid ourselves of bitterness. "Let all bitterness and wrath and anger and clamor [perpetual animosity, resentment, strife, fault-finding] and slander be put away from you, along with every kind of malice [all spitefulness, verbal abuse, malevolence]. Be kind and helpful to one another, tender-hearted [compassionate, understanding], forgiving one another [readily and freely], just as God in Christ also forgave you" (Ephesians 4:31–32 AMP).

Questions to ponder:

+ *What have you sowed—and may still be sowing—that has attributed to the harvest of bitterness in you and your relationships?*

+ *Do you recognize/realize you are serving gods other than the one and only Yahweh, and so have suffered or are suffering from bitterness in your life?*

+ *Is there any disobedience to God that is causing bitterness in your life?*

+ *Are you feeding bitterness with your words, actions, and attitude?*

+ *Are you willing to let bitterness alter your book of life?*

PART 3

VISION CORRECTION

11

REPENTANCE

A Divine Exchange

True repentance will entirely change you, the bias of your souls will be changed, then you will delight in God, in Christ, in His Law, and in His people.

—*George Whitefield*

C hanging lenses requires repentance. Repentance is defined as "a change that takes place in one's life as a result of the Holy Spirit's work to illumine one's consciousness to the state of sin in the presence of a Holy God."[1]

Any taints of a person's lenses are a deviation from the original lens of love. The images we see through tainted lenses are no longer original images; they have become distorted, blemished, and blurry. The images we see of God, ourselves, and others through tainted lenses are not the true images God created and intended them to be but rather false and warped images. To restore the original images, we need to first recognize our lenses are tainted, and then correct them.

My prayer is that the Holy Spirit will shine His light and illuminate your consciousness to recognize the lenses you wear when viewing God, yourself, and others.

As a mother, I want to raise my children to be responsible—or at least as responsible as I am. My desire and expectations of raising responsible children clashed frequently with those of my husband. We were not on the same page, each of us seeing things from our own backgrounds.

I grew up in a poor rural county in China. I raised pigs and chickens and helped to clean up house besides going to school. I took care of my little brother, regardless that I was a child myself. My husband grew up in Brazil and the United States in a middleclass family. His childhood was fully dedicated to schooling, with only minimum chores he had to do to get by. My expectation for raising responsible children is to assign chores, while my husband is more lenient about it.

From time to time, I would become frustrated with the amount of housework I needed to do. I expected my kids to take on more of the tasks as this would be good training for them. Somehow, my expectations caused tension between me and my husband. Finally, I brought it to the Lord. "Lord, do I see this situation with tainted lenses?"

I was reminded of what I'd said to myself: I don't like the aspect of Chinese culture when parents treat their children as their social security, bringing them up so they can look after them when they get old. I resented this aspect of Chinese culture while growing up. I felt children were not being loved but were rather being used.

When the Lord reminded me of this, I was surprised. I said, "Lord, are you saying that I want my daughters to be *useful*? My heart's intention is to train them to be responsible."

Sometimes, we don't even know our own heart. I repented for perpetuating the very aspect of Chinese culture I'd resented. I released my children from my expectations of being useful to me. Since then, I am not so anxious about the housework.

Repentance has become a pathway of transformation for me. Through repentance, I bring old things to the cross and through the blood of Jesus, new things come. "Therefore, if anyone is in Christ, he is a new creation; old things have passed away; behold, all things have become new" (2 Corinthians 5:17 NKJV). Through repentance, I experience the divine exchange at the foot of the cross: the death of the old for the birth of the new.

Repentance is to take responsibility. When I recognize my lenses are tainted and deviate from the lens of love, it is my responsibility to take them off and replace them with new lenses. Blaming others for our own distorted lenses is not taking responsibility. It negates the power of transformation in one's life.

Repentance is also to renew our mindset. We repent from our own perspective and our own ways and turn to God's ways and His perspective. "That ye put off concerning the former conversation the old man, which is corrupt according to the deceitful lusts; and be renewed in the spirit of your mind; and that ye put on the new man, which after God is created in righteousness and true holiness" (Ephesians 4:22–24 KJV).

Questions to ponder:

✦ *When was the last time you repented?*

✦ *How has repentance changed the way you see God, self, and others?*

12

FORGIVENESS

The Key to Unlock the Prison Door

We must develop and maintain the capacity to forgive.
He who is devoid of the power to forgive is devoid of the
power to love. There is some good in the worst of us and
some evil in the best of us. When we discover this,
we are less prone to hate our enemies.

—*Martin Luther King, Jr.*

Many years ago, I enjoyed a close friendship with a lady who went to the same church as me. The community in which we were both involved went through a fierce conflict; people took sides and some were very hurt. I said words that hurt my friend, although I wasn't aware of it at the time.

Sometime later, I repeatedly had dreams about this lady. I knew I needed to ask for her forgiveness for the hurt I'd caused. I agonized for a while and feared she wouldn't answer my call. I finally plucked up the courage and called her; I'd asked my husband to be by my side to support me. When my friend answered, I apologized to her and asked for her forgiveness. She didn't say much on the phone but from that day onwards, I didn't dream about her anymore. I didn't know if she accepted my repentance or not; that was between her and God. The most important part was that I had peace in my heart.

True forgiveness is demonstrated in our ability to talk about the people who hurt us or a hurtful experience with peace—the peace that doesn't demand to get even, the peace that enables us to speak well of those who hurt us, the peace of being able to strike up a conversation with those people rather than avoiding them when we meet them in a grocery store. In *that* kind of peace is the absence of fear, absence of offense, absence of judgment, absence of bitterness and anger, absence of darkness, and the absence of hatred.

Trudy Bourgeois wrote an article for *Huffpost* entitled *The Greatest Gift—To: You and I, From: Nelson Mandela* in which she said, "Any man who could spend 27 years unjustly imprisoned and then say this: *'As I walked out the door toward the gate that would lead to my freedom, I knew if I didn't leave my bitterness and hatred behind, I'd still be in prison.'* THAT is a leader. THAT is a person who could see beyond himself. And THAT is a man who understood **the absolute power** of forgiveness."[1]

For people who have a difficult time forgiving, the best remedy is to examine the lenses they wear. Our reaction to a person, to words, or a circumstance reflect the lenses we have.

Jesus' responses and reactions proved His lens of love in viewing those who persecuted Him. When He was faced with accusations, slander, hatred, and even death, He offered forgiveness. In the most difficult time of His earthly life—being hung on the cross—He asked the Father to forgive those who had accused Him and put Him on the cross. "Father, forgive them; for they do not know what they are doing" (Luke 23:34).

People's treatment of and words about Him as he hung in terrible suffering further tested his forgiveness. "And even the rulers were sneering at Him, saying, 'He saved others; let Him save Himself if this is the Christ of God, His Chosen One'" (Luke 23:35). But He didn't talk back to them. He didn't respond to the soldiers' mockery as they called to Him to save Himself if He was indeed the King of the Jews. He didn't respond to the verbal abuse of one of the criminals hanging on a cross beside him: "Are You not the Christ? Save Yourself and us!" (Luke 23:39). He did not waste one ounce of His energy on taking offense or in bitterness, hatred, complaining, criticism, or unforgiveness. Instead, He remained firm, expecting God's promise to be fulfilled, as He'd told His disciples earlier, ". . . the Son of Man must be delivered into the hands of sinful men, and be crucified, and the third day rise again" (Luke 24:7). His silence on the cross proved His forgiveness.

He did respond to the criminal hanging at His other side who cried, "Jesus, remember me when You come in Your kingdom!" (Luke 23:42). Jesus promised to meet that criminal in Paradise.

The very first time the word *forgive* appears in the Bible is in the book of Genesis. Joseph's brothers had sold him to be a slave in a foreign land when he was a young boy, deceiving their father, Jacob, by telling him animals had devoured his beloved son. Joseph spent years in an Egyptian jail because of the injustices his brothers had done to him. Eventually, it was Joseph who saved the entire tribe of Israel from famine.

When Jacob died, Joseph and his brothers buried him in the land of Canaan and mourned there for seven days. With Jacob gone, the brothers were afraid. "When Joseph's brothers saw that their father was dead, they said, 'What if Joseph holds a grudge against us and pays us back for all the wrongs we did to him?' So they sent word to Joseph, saying, 'Your father left these instructions before he died: "This is what you are to say to Joseph: I ask you to forgive your brothers the sins and the wrongs they committed in treating you so badly." Now please forgive the sins of the servants of the God of your father.' When their message came to him, Joseph wept" (Genesis 50:15–17 NIV).

It took more than twenty years for Joseph's brothers to ask for forgiveness. It took that many years for Joseph's lenses to change from *you intended evil against me* to *God meant it for good*, and to change from *me* to the lens of *God*. "But Joseph said to them, 'Don't be afraid. Am I in the place of God? You intended to harm me, but God intended it for good to accomplish what is now being done, the saving of many lives. So then, don't be afraid. I will provide for you and your children.' And he reassured them and spoke kindly to them" (Genesis 50:19–21 NIV).

It took some time for me to forgive the company and individuals who made the decision to demote me. It took some time for me to see that *God meant it for good.*

Forgiveness is to remove tainted lenses and see God, others, and self with a new set of lenses. When people recognize the tainted lenses through which they view others, a profound change takes place—a change from *it is all his or her fault* to *oh, it could be my perspective or my judgment.*

As the table turns, so does the responsibility. When it is another person's fault, we may remain bitter and distant. When we discover *our* view of others is tainted, we can take action to remove the taints in our lenses. When we replace our tainted lenses with the lens of love, forgiveness becomes easier. Forgiveness is the most effective weapon against offense, judgment, and bitterness.

Forgiveness has a tremendous healing effect on our bodies. In an article for CBN News entitled *The Deadly Consequences of Unforgiveness*[2], Lorie Johnson writes, "According to Dr. Steven Standiford, chief of surgery at the Cancer Treatment Centers of America, refusing to forgive makes people sick and keeps them that way. With that in mind, forgiveness therapy is now being used to help treat diseases, such as cancer. . . .

Of all cancer patients, 61 percent have forgiveness issues, and of those, more than half are severe, according to research by Dr. Michael Barry, a pastor and the author of the book, *The Forgiveness Project*. 'Harboring these negative emotions, this anger and hatred, creates a state of chronic anxiety,' he said. 'Chronic anxiety very predictably produces excess adrenaline and cortisol, which deplete the production of natural killer cells, which is your body's foot soldier in the fight against cancer,' he explained. . . . Barry said most people don't realize what a burden anger and hatred were until they let them go."

Forgiveness may have to be by layers if our emotions are buried deep. Meditating on past hurts, wounds, and injustices—real or perceived—deepens the impression of unforgiveness, bitterness, or even hatred. We need to forgive one aspect, forgive another aspect, and then forgive yet another aspect—even of the same traumatic event or memory—until we have perfect peace.

Jesus confirmed this to Peter when he asked him about forgiveness. "Then Peter came and said to Him, 'Lord, how often shall my brother sin against me and I forgive him? Up to seven times?' Jesus said to him, 'I do not say to you, up to seven times, but up to seventy times seven'" (Matthew 18:21–22).

Andrea is a friend of mine; here is her forgiveness story. Andrea's family were immigrants from Taiwan to the United States. Her father's brother did not have any children. He and his wife often fought because of this. Her father really loved his brother and wanted to see him happy. When Andrea was about three years old, her parents decided to give her to her uncle, to be his daughter. In her parents' view, they had another boy; they were willing to give away their daughter to her father's brother.

After a long journey by train and bus, Andrea was delivered to her uncle, and left there by her father. One month later, a telegram was delivered to her father saying she cried a lot and her father should come and take her back. Soon after

Andrea returned to her own parents; her uncle was killed in a car accident. This news devastated her father. Perhaps it was because God knew what lay ahead that she was sent back.

Andrea didn't have any memory of these happenings. But she could never understand why she had always been so driven to be top of her class. She would feel a totally worthless failure when her grade didn't place her in the top three. Whenever she was praised for her good grades by her teacher, she would lift her head high, as if her worth was validated.

In her college years, Andrea was introduced to God and Jesus. She believed Him for all His promises. She forgave her parents for the anger, fights, and violence she had witnessed as a child.

Miraculously, her father accepted Jesus at a church service. Hallelujah! Andrea was so excited to see a new creation of her father. Unfortunately, she still witnessed his explosive anger and sometimes heard his mean words. She realized everything about her father irritated her. Her father sensed it and shouted at her, "God has forgiven me, why can't you?" She was speechless; she knew she should forgive and forget but she couldn't. Her mind still meditated on her father's faults, his destructive behaviors still floating constantly in her thoughts.

One day, in a casual conversation between her parents and their friends, Andrea overheard a story about a three-year-old girl who had been given away and then taken back. She finally connected the dots. With this new piece of information, her heart was filled with anger and resentment. She didn't want to speak to her father. Sensing her bitterness, he shouted angrily, "My brother was a good man; he loved us so much and gave the best to our families in the most difficult seasons of our lives. He gave us so much. I loved him so I gave him my daughter; that was the best thing that I could do. What was wrong with that?" Andrea couldn't hold her tears and ran to her room, weeping.

THE LENS OF LOVE

In that time and culture, such an event would be considered normal or even noble. But seeking right in all the wrongs wouldn't help liberate her from all her bitterness and hatred. It was up to Andrea and her faith in God to walk out of the abyss of unworthiness.

Andrea recounted her conversation with God. She heard that "God so loved the world, that He gave His only begotten Son, that whoever believes in Him shall not perish, but have eternal life" (John 3:16). In her mind she heard, "Your father really loved his brother so he gave you." Andrea immediately shouted back, "But I'm not Jesus!"

She needed some help in sorting all this out; she couldn't stand being consumed by anger and bitterness any longer. In a prayer session with a prayer minister, the intercessor asked her, "Are you willing to forgive your father for giving you away and for all the pain you are carrying?"

Andrea answered hesitantly, "I am willing."

"I am asking you to put on the lens of Jesus, to look at your father with the lens of Jesus, and tell me what you see."

Silence for a few minutes.

"He is so frightened," Andrea eventually said, "full of guilt and shame. He is curled up like a ball in the corner."

She didn't know how to respond to this as her father was so dominating, easily angered, and scary to be around. In Jesus' eyes, he was afraid, scared, bound. Jesus had compassion for him.

Speaking out "I forgive" might not have released the weight in her heart completely, but it was a good start. Seeing her father as scared, fearful, and bound didn't justify all the wrongs and pain, but Andrea was able to have compassion for him. That was the lens of love, which God created in us in the beginning.

Forgiveness and the lens of love can lead us to perfect peace.

Sue Lin is a leader with many skills and gifting. She would tell newcomers to a Fortune 500 transportation company where she worked, "I am very wary of people who are ambitious and eager to grab titles and positions." Over time, some people in the organization noticed a pattern in Sue Lin's leadership style. She would come to every department and declare war: these are the things that are not working well and here is my proposal to fix them.

Very soon, she became the leader of several key departments. Some people started to become offended by her forceful leadership style. Some people judged her. "She is so fake. She tells people to watch out for ambitious people who are after titles and positions, and yet she is the most ambitious among us all."

Sue Lin was an effective reformer; she deeply believed that the changes she implemented were best for the organization. However, that gift was only appreciated by her boss. Many of her team members worked with her on a superficial level only, while they secretly looked for an opportunity to work elsewhere. Jealousy and bitterness brewed in their hearts. I had a brief encounter with Sue Lin and a taste of her abrasive words of correction in front of a group of people.

In Sue Lin's case, the people who are offended, judging, and bitter have the tainted lenses. It is not their job to make Sue Lin see her tainted lenses or abrasive leadership styles, or to change Sue Lin. If I am the one who is offended, who is judging, and who is bitter inside, it is my responsibility to identify my tainted lenses, and to take them off and put on the lens of love. That was what I did.

I chose to forgive her for her abrasive remarks.

I repented for being prideful.

I replaced my lens of pride with the lens of love.

I asked God to show me who Sue Lin is through His lens of love.

I saw a woman with boldness, determination, and relentless drive, pushing through the boundaries of old structures; and I saw her heart for something greater. I realized I can be on her side, pushing for and not against her for the common goal.

To this day, we are still on good terms, and can talk and laugh together.

Questions to ponder:

+ *Do you hold any offense against anyone (God, others, or yourself)?*
+ *Is there anyone you need to forgive? What for?*
+ *Are you judging someone you need to forgive?*
+ *Do you know forgiveness starts from your mouth—that you need to confess it with your mouth and then believe it in your heart?*

13

THE STATUE OF ABRAHAM LINCOLN

Friendship with God

Smart men walked on the moon, daring men walked on the ocean floor, but wise men walk with God.

—Leonard Ravenhill

I desired an intimate relationship with Jesus. In February 2010, I decided to do a seven-day bridal fast. The purpose of the fast was to draw closer to God and His heart. During the fast, I immersed myself in His presence; I danced to Him and with Him; I communed with Him through prayer and writing as I so wanted to be His bride. Here is my journal entry from the second day of the fast:

Today, I found a prayer room near my daughter's school by surprise. While waiting to pick her up, I was so delighted to spend one hour in this quiet place meeting with my Lord. Here, I took a communion in remembering His body and blood. God showed me a picture (in my mind's eyes) where

He picked me (a little girl) and tossed me up and down and picked me up when I fell down. I heard laughter. We were having a lot of fun. When I surveyed the ground as I fell downwards, I thought to myself: He is always there to pick me up, so I have nothing to be afraid of. Immediately, I start to fly fearlessly.

The God I saw was fun, protective, and safe.

One year later, my husband and I enrolled in the supernatural school of ministry with a church in Arizona. Every video lesson was life changing. One of the lessons was called *Father's Ladder* by Danny Silk from Bethel Church. Following Danny's instructions to experience it fully, with eyes closed we entered the Father's throne room at the guidance of the Holy Spirit. Everyone was weeping.

This was the first time in my life I'd entered the throne room. I saw the statue of Abraham Lincoln. I really didn't know why, but I wept. I knew the statue of Abraham Lincoln wasn't the true representation of the Father God. The statue looks cold, giant, and unapproachable.

This picture said a lot about my view of Father God. Perhaps there was sadness in the distance between the Father and me. Perhaps I needed to repent and forgive more. I thought I had done enough repentance and forgiveness. But it seemed more was needed. The sound of sobbing in the room told me I wasn't the only one experiencing this. It was humbling to know my journey of knowing God had only just began.

In Exodus chapter 32, the people of Israel saw with their own eyes how God had performed signs, wonders, and miracles to bring them out of Egypt and slavery. Moses was the leader and mediator between God and the people of Israel. When Moses went up a mountain to visit with God, the people of Israel started to doubt the presence of God. After a while, when there was still no sign of Moses, they made a god for themselves out of gold and jewels. They desperately needed a god to guide and protect them. They had a God who met all their needs, but they didn't know Him. There was distance between them and God. They would stand at a distance to worship God's presence, which was a pillar of cloud at the entrance of the tent where Moses met with God.

Moses knew God for who He really is and God had proclaimed His names to him. "And the Lord passed by before him, and proclaimed, The Lord, The Lord God, merciful and gracious, longsuffering, and abundant in goodness and truth, keeping mercy for thousands, forgiving iniquity and transgression and sin, and that will by no means clear the guilty; visiting the iniquity of the fathers upon the children, and upon the children's children, unto the third and to the fourth generation" (Exodus 34:6–7 KJV).

God is compassionate and gracious, and He forgave the sin of idolatry when Moses interceded for the Israelites. God is holy and His holiness requires the price of sin to be paid. His love and faithfulness are manifested through forgiveness of wickedness, rebellion, and sin for thousands of generations, yet He only remembers the iniquity of the fathers to the third or fourth generations.

Moses not only knows God's nature and character; he also prayed to know God's way. His prayer was answered. "My presence shall go with thee, and I will give thee rest" (Exodus 33:14 KJV). In God's presence, we get to know His ways and receive rest.

Knowing God for who He really is and walking with Him in His presence is the cure to idolatry. Jesus is the image of the invisible God (Colossians 1:15) and he who has seen Jesus has seen the Father (John 14:9). Therefore, having a relationship with Jesus and knowing Him is knowing God.

What does it mean to know God for who He really is? It is like knowing a good friend. You have a friend; they may have a good reputation; you know what they do for a living. You may know the highlights of their lives if you follow them on social media. But until you spend time with this person, your knowledge of them is on a superficial level. When you spend time with that person and talk with them, you start to know their likes and dislikes, their desires, dreams, failures, struggles, and even heartaches. You bond with that person by eating together, playing together, doing things together, with tears and laughter, and even through times of misunderstanding and reconciliation. Your friend may sometimes get tired or have their own issues and is no longer available to be a friend anymore. But God is always available.

My friendship with God continues to grow and in this growing process it has gone through several stages:

1. Head knowledge: my love for Him expressed in obedience to the Law. I consider myself a servant; He blesses me as I serve Him.

2. Experience: my love for Him expressed in surrendering my will to Him, either involuntarily or voluntarily. His love does not depend on my work. He still blesses me even while I am trying to figure out who I am in Christ. As I help others to get free from their junk, as I serve the orphans and bring good news to those who don't know Him, I discover my authority and power in Christ and the gifting He has given me.

3. Oneness with God: body, soul and spirit. I am still growing in my friendship with God.

Questions to ponder:

+ *How well do you know God?*
+ *Are you walking in His way?*
+ *What are some of the ways you know God intimately?*

14

GOD'S WORD

The Truth Has Set Us Free

All Scripture is inspired by God and profitable for teaching,
for reproof, for correction, for training in righteousness;
so that the man of God may be adequate,
equipped for every good work.

—*2 Timothy 3:16–17*

The number one remedy to correct our tainted lenses is the Word of God. God's Word is like the standard eye chart. The taints of our lenses will be revealed when we measure our eyesight against the standard eye chart—the Word of God.

My husband and I were in a discipleship meeting with our pastor. He asked me what verse I was mediating that week. It was Philippians 4:6–7: "Be anxious for nothing, but in everything by prayer and supplication with thanksgiving let your requests be made known to God. And the peace of God, which surpasses all comprehension, will guard your hearts and your minds in Christ Jesus."

Since I'd started meditating on this verse, I had made some significant changes in my heart. I used to be very anxious when my husband traveled for work. He travels at least one week out of each month. I felt like a single parent and prayed (complained) for him to travel less, so both of us could share the parenting responsibilities.

The lenses through which I saw myself were *weak* and *I need help from people.* My mom comes to help me when my husband goes on a business trip. Yes, I am so blessed to have her help. However, I still experience anxiety when my husband travels, especially when my younger daughter gets sick. After months or even years of praying (complaining), his travel schedule hasn't changed much.

When I started to meditate on this verse, I realized I was *not* anxious for nothing, and my prayers were *not* with thanksgiving. I did make my requests known to God, but with plenty of grumbling.

One day, as my eyes focused on these verses, I thought about how to give thanks. I started to thank God for His provision through my husband's job and travels. I thanked God for our two beautiful daughters who love God. As I continued on the journey of thankfulness, the peace of God started to settle in. A couple of weeks later, when my mom told me she would be going on vacation at the same time my husband would be away on his travels, I told her, "No problem, I'll be OK." I released her from her duty of helping me. I had confidence that God and I would make it through together.

God's Word shifted my lens from *I am weak and need people's help* to *God and I will make it together.*

Questions to ponder:

+ *Is God's Word relevant to your daily life?*
+ *When was the last time God's Word removed taints from your lenses?*

15

HEAVEN'S VANTAGE POINT

Seeing beyond the Natural

*When a storm is coming, all other birds seek shelter. The Eagle
alone, avoids the storm by flying above it. So, in the storms
of life . . . may your heart soar like an Eagle.*

—Unknown

An eagle flies high and can reach an altitude of 10,000
feet. It has sharp eyes and can see very far, able to spot
its prey from miles away. When an eagle soars in the
sky, it glides effortlessly. From its high vantage point, it flies
above the resistance of the crowded world.

How often do you hear this from Christians: "I am doing
something great for God but I'm encountering so many attacks
and I have to push through so much resistance." Often, opposition doesn't come from the enemy but rather from our tainted
lenses. The reason we continually struggle with resistance is
that we still dwell on our worldly knowledge and understanding. We haven't risen above the storm line so we aren't able
to see from the heavenly vantage point. We need to switch

from seeing from an earthly perspective to seeing through the lens of heaven.

Have you ever put yourself in the Word you read and meditate on and see yourself act a part in it? I am inviting you to read Isaiah 40:31; put yourself in the Word and act it out.

"Yet those who wait for the Lord will gain new strength; they will mount up with wings like eagles, they will run and not get tired, they will walk and not become weary."

When I immersed myself in this verse, I saw myself with wings ascending to the sky, far above all the busyness of the world. Like an eagle I was flying, my feet moving without any resistance because I had entered a resistance-free zone; it is a place where my Lord reigns and I surrender to His Lordship completely. It is a place where I rest from my ways and follow His directions.

There is no better passage than Ephesians 2:6 to describe the heavenly vantage point, as God has "raised us up with Him, and seated us with Him in the heavenly places in Christ Jesus." At this very moment, we have been raised and are seated with Him in the heavenly places in Christ Jesus. The work of being raised from death to life has finished. We walk on the earth at the same time as we are seated with Christ in heavenly places.

Many of us either don't know or forget that we dwell on earth and in heavenly places simultaneously. We are multidimensional beings. The enemy cannot get to me since I am in Christ. Jesus is my fortress, my protection; the enemy doesn't have a chance to harm me as Christ has victory over the enemy.

The clause "in Christ Jesus" means Christ is the center. We are crucified with Him; we are new creatures, and we live a new life by faith in Jesus as children of God. "Therefore if anyone is in Christ, he is a new creature" (2 Corinthians 5:17). "Be renewed in the spirit of your mind, and put on the new self, which in the likeness of God has been created in righteousness and holiness of the truth" (Ephesians 4:23–24).

"But as many as received Him, to them He gave the right to become children of God, even to those who believe in his name" (John 1:12).

In our communication with God, we come to a place of peace. I call it a happy place. My happy place looks like a peaceful beach; Jesus holds my hand as we stroll along the beach. One time, I was sitting on the Father's lap and He was showing me maps. Another time, I was riding on a rocket with Jesus. He was showing me the planet, stars, and universe. You can argue that all these may be in my imagination. This argument denies the reality of imagination.

During one of the trainings on inner healing we conducted in Hong Kong, we led a short exercise with a group of people. We read Psalm 23 to them after which the group of people closed their physical eyes and imagined themselves in the pictures or actions of Psalm 23:

"The Lord is my shepherd,
I shall not want.
He makes me lie down in green pastures;
He leads me beside quiet waters.
He restores my soul;
He guides me in the paths of righteousness
For His name's sake.

Even though I walk through the valley of the shadow of death,
I fear no evil, for You are with me;
Your rod and Your staff, they comfort me.
You prepare a table before me in the presence of my enemies;
You have anointed my head with oil;
My cup overflows.
Surely goodness and lovingkindness will follow me all the days of my life,
And I will dwell in the house of the Lord forever."

At the end of the exercise, we discussed the outcome. One person said she was sitting across from God the Father; a banquet table was between them. The Father said to her, "Eat and drink; I have defeated the enemy." She looked at the Father and He smiled at her; His gaze focused fully on her as if nothing could distract Him. She sat with Him, eating and drinking. There is no trace of fear in her and no trace of fear around her.

Another person stomped her feet at the end of the exercise. She explained her actions to us. "After the feast with the Lord, He asked me to stomp my feet and the enemy left at the sound of my stomping. Isn't that cool?"

We all have imagination. This particular exercise is intended to activate our imagination by putting yourself in the Bible verses and letting the Holy Spirit direct you into an encounter with the Author of the Word. We call this sanctified imagination.

There are two kinds of imagination: Godly and ungodly. In the beginning, God formed man out of the dust. The Hebrew word for *form* is *va-yatzar*, or *yatsar* meaning to form, or fashion. "Then the Lord God formed man of dust from the ground, and breathed into his nostrils the breath of life; and man became a living being" (Genesis 2:7). Through Godly imagination, God formed man out of the dust according to His image.

In the Book of Exodus, Aaron fashioned a golden calf after gathering the gold from the people of Israel, with the Hebrew word *yatsar* describing what he did. Through ungodly imagination, Aaron fashioned the idol. "And he received them at their hand, and fashioned it with a graving tool, after he had made it a molten calf: and they said, These be thy gods, O Israel, which brought thee up out of the land of Egypt" (Exodus 32:4 KJV).

In Genesis 6:5, the Hebrew word for *intent* or *imagination* of the thoughts is *yê-ṣer* or *yetser*, the root of which is *yatsar* meaning a form, framing, purpose. "There were giants in the earth in those days; and also after that, when the sons of God came in unto the daughters of men, and they bare children to them, the same became mighty men which were of old, men of renown. And God saw that the wickedness of man was great in the earth, and that every imagination of the thoughts of his heart was only evil continually" (Genesis 6:4–5).

Man had intermarried with the fallen angels and through ungodly imagination man's heart intended to do evil continually on the earth. God brought a flood to destroy everything and everyone except Noah's family.

When God created the earth, the word *create* meant He made everything in His imagination. I am made in His image. I can create with my imagination.

Another prime example of godly and ungodly imaginations is the story of how David and others faced the giant, Goliath. Godly imaginations based on and consistent with the Word of God result in faith and courage. Ungodly imaginations result in fear and death. Flesh and fleshly desires drive ungodly imaginations.

The Bible describes the Philistine giant, Goliath. The weight of his coat was five thousand shekels of brass and his spear's head weighed six hundred shekels of iron. The Philistine challenged the armies of Israel to fight; whoever lost the battle would become the servant of the other party.

King Saul and the Israelite army heard the Philistine's words and were dismayed and very afraid. The Israelite army had a vivid imagination of what the Philistine was going to do to them. In the presence of the giant, they felt very small, not even measuring up to his spear. Their ungodly imaginations led to fear and defeat before the battle even started.

But when David heard Goliath's defiling words, his reaction was very different. "Then David spoke to the men who were standing by him, saying, 'What will be done for the man who kills this Philistine and takes away the reproach from Israel?

THE LENS OF LOVE

For who is this uncircumcised Philistine, that he should taunt the armies of the living God?'" (1 Samuel 17:26).

In David's mind, the battle was between an uncircumcised Philistine and God. His imagination was full of the greatness of God and anything that was against God would undoubtedly fail. The foundation of his imagination was the faithfulness of God. It came from his personal experience of shepherding and of how God had delivered him again and again. His Godly imagination led him to face the giant Goliath without fear and kill him with a stone from his sling.

In our daily lives, a big part of our thought life is imagination. When we suddenly lose contact with a close friend with whom we are used to regularly connecting through texts and phone calls, our imagination starts to run wild: why isn't she returning my calls and my texts? Is she OK? When the doctor says, "I am so sorry to tell you that the biopsy we did is positive and the tissue is cancerous," our mind starts to run wild. What? How could this happen to me? Does this mean I am near death? In our imagination, cancer is an untreatable disease and means a death sentence. Or when the doctor says, "We need to send you to hospice and there is nothing more we can do," the word *hospice* is like a pronouncement of death because our imagination links it with death.

We have the responsibility to submit our imagination to God and ask Him to sanctify it. When there is an ungodly imagination infused with fear and defeat, we need to bring it to the Lord and ask the Holy Spirit: is this in alignment with the Word of God or is it against the Word of God? If the answer we hear from God is "No, it's not in alignment," we can reject the ungodly imagination and give it no space in our mind. This is why it is so important for us to know the Word of God.

We prayed for a woman, Ruth. She told us that at nighttime she could hear the sound of steps around the bed as if someone was walking on the carpet. She could feel an evil presence pressing into her face. She grew up with a mom who studied demonology and visited horror houses and buildings. She came to know the Lord in her thirties, yet the fear of demons still gripped her. In all her imaginations (thoughts), she saw demons and feared what harm they could do to her.

She repented of her fear of demons and forgave her mom for teaching her the ways of the demons. We asked her to go to the scene where she'd encountered a demonic presence. At the prompting of the Holy Spirit, she asked for a weapon from Jesus to get rid of the demonic presence. She saw that Jesus gave her the Bible. He was asking her to speak the Word of God to rebuke the demons. As she declared the Word by faith, the demons fled. No longer plagued by the ungodly imaginations, she now saw herself with the power and authority from God to fight against evil.

For the first time in her life, Ruth understood this truth: "For though we walk in the flesh, we do not war after the flesh: (for the weapons of our warfare are not carnal, but mighty through God to the pulling down of strong holds;) casting down imaginations, and every high thing that exalteth itself against the knowledge of God, and bringing into captivity every thought to the obedience of Christ" (2 Corinthians 10:3–5 KJV).

Questions to ponder:

+ *Do the thoughts or images in your imagination reflect your tainted lenses or the lens of the love?*

+ *When was the last time you rejected ungodly imagination and gained peace?*

16

DIVINE REVELATIONS

Prophecy and Dreams

*He said, "Hear now My words: If there is a prophet among
you, I, the Lord, shall make Myself known to him in a vision.
I shall speak with him in a dream.*

—Numbers 12:6

As spiritual beings, we know God by His Word, by communication with Him through prayer, and by doing life with fellow brothers and sisters in the setting of community and family. We also get to know God through the divine revelation of Jesus through the Holy Spirit. Divine revelation includes prophecies, dreams and visions.

Merriam-Webster's definition of the word *prophecy* is:

1. An inspired utterance of a prophet.

2. The function or vocation of a prophet, *specifically* the inspired declaration of divine will and purpose.

3. A prediction of something to come.

I have received many prophecies over the last ten years. Some prophecies spoke into my identity as a child of God. Some helped me to see how God sees me. Some revealed God's love and so sparked hope in me. Some prophecies spoke of things to come and not yet fulfilled. I have received several prophecies about writing books and one of these prophecies is about to be fulfilled.

I had the lens of abandonment and the lens of self-reliance since I was a child. My family didn't have much when I grew up. I started to work around the house when I was seven or eight years old, fetching water from the well, gathering grass to feed the chickens and pigs, and collecting saffron flowers to sell for money. I even took care of my younger brother when my parents were away at work.

My father went away to work on the construction of a railroad; he was absent from my life for many years. My mom took my brother to visit him for a few months at a time, leaving me with my maternal grandma. When my father came back, I called him uncle because I didn't know him at all.

When I heard stories from my family about my childhood, I always felt I'd had a miserable childhood, was made to grow up too early, and bore too many burdens. This has always driven me to work harder to make a better life.

After I was married with children, a pastor friend prophesied over me, "Your life is a life of miracles. God has given you many miracles. Your life is a miracle, your children are miracles, and your marriage is a miracle." This prophecy directly contradicted *my* view of my life, which was miserable and difficult. The prophecy spoke God's view of my life. As the pastor prophesied, many pictures passed through my mind.

The first series of pictures was of the time when I was in my mother's womb. Mom and Dad were riding horses, traveling to work. Mom was pregnant with me. They had to cross a river over a very narrow bridge. It wasn't much of a bridge, only two lines of wooden planks laid across the river. The water underneath was running fast. My dad's horse jumped over to the other side. My mom's horse started to jump, but something unexpected happened. One of her horse's legs slipped off the wooden planks. My dad held the rope and used all his strength to pull the horse. If the horse jumped over, then both mother and baby would be safe; if not, both mother and baby would fall into the cold running water. The horse jumped over as my dad, shouting, pulled the rope. Both mom and baby were safe.

The second series of pictures told the story of a time when a lost baby was found. A young couple drove a horse carriage as they moved from one mountainous village to another. There was a massive bump in the road, which they did not see. They hit it and suddenly the baby held in the wife's bosom flew out of her arms. The couple didn't know where the baby had landed. All of their belongings that had been piled on the carriage were scattered around. They frantically looked everywhere for the baby, even underneath their belongings, but the baby was nowhere to be found. After they'd searched for a long time, they finally found the bundle inside a bush. The baby wasn't hurt or crying; in fact, she was still sleeping. It was a miracle the baby was alive and well after this ordeal.

I was that baby.

As these pictures passed through my mind's eye, I only saw the protection of God. At the time those events happened, I obviously didn't even know Him. And yet, He was there to protect me. I am alive and well today because of Him. Gratitude filled my heart. When I saw God as who He is—loving, kind, and protector of my life—the taints on my lenses faded away.

One of the ways God speaks to me is through dreams. After we moved to Hong Kong, I learned to interpret dreams for others through hearing God. I also hear God by interpreting my own dreams. I hear His instruction, correction, encouragement, and warning through dreams. Like many spiritual gifts, interpreting dreams is a gift God deposits in us and we become good at it when we practice a lot. Most of my dreams are like parables in the Bible, telling a story and illustrating a point in picture form. The elements in the dream are most often symbolic.

In January 2016, I had a dream in which I was destined to marry an old man. In the dream, there was an old man who was very famous and wealthy. My mom and dad wanted me to marry him, although I was much younger than him. Somebody took him to a meeting and all the people there cheered when he arrived. He had invented a spa chair with water automatically springing out for massage—the first of its kind in the world.

The interpretation of the dream was as follows: the old man in the dream represented God, with all his fame and wealth. Mom and dad approving the marriage spoke of the generational calling for godly blessings and inheritance in my life. In this dream, *to marry* symbolizes an intimate relationship with the Lord Almighty. God desired my heart and for me to have an intimate relationship with Him. He is the God of all creation and the God of all provision. He is to be praised and greatly honored (indicated by all the people cheering). He will pour down His blessing, cleansing, and comfort into my life (indicated by the spa chair) and I will do the same to others. In this intimate relationship, the world will see the original and unique person whom God has created me to be. Knowing God's heart desire for intimacy with me is comforting. I see His kindness and goodness through this dream.

In July 2019, I had a dream about my younger daughter. She was a third-grade elementary student and insisted on going to school by herself. I told her to go with her older brother but she didn't want to listen and went by herself. I was concerned for her safety. At the time, I was at an emotional high, with everything going well in my life. My reliance on God was giving way to my reliance on my own strength. In this dream, God was reminding me to be humble and partner with Him.

Although the dream appeared to be for my daughter, I knew she symbolized me. The older brother was Jesus. It was humbling to know that my journey in the school of life was only at the elementary level. God was inviting me to walk with Him instead of walking alone. This dream corrected my lenses on self-reliance and revealed the new lens of walking with Jesus to reach safe places.

Questions to ponder:

+ *How have prophecies changed your tainted lenses?*
+ *How have interpreted dreams changed your tainted lenses?*

17

GOD ENCOUNTERS

Transformation in the Presence

*One encounter with Jesus Christ is enough
to change you, instantly, forever.*

—Luis Palau

O ne encounter with God can dispose of our tainted
lenses and replace them with a new set of lenses.

My maternal grandfather exerted control and
dominance over my grandmother. My grandmother would
cook for my grandfather and serve him. She was a person
of service; she loved to help her children when they needed.
However, she would be punished by my grandfather for going
away to support her children.

When I was about seven years old, my parents left me
with my grandmother for a month. Grandfather didn't like
little girls; he only liked boys. It was prevalent for parents or
grandparents to favor boys over girls in China at that time
because they believed that boys would carry the family name
forward.

137

One afternoon, I was looking for my grandmother and walked into the courtyard outside their house. The sight in front of me terrified me. My grandfather was on top of my grandmother, his hands around her throat as he choked her. Her face was turning purple. Out of fear, I screamed loudly, "Help!" My uncle, who lived next door, ran over and pulled my grandfather away.

During my journey of inner healing, I asked Jesus this question many times: where were you when my grandfather was choking my grandmother? I didn't hear any answer the first two times I asked. The third time, He showed me a vision: Jesus was there, in between my grandfather and my grandmother. He was taking all the choking, all the beating. I dissolved in a puddle of tears at this and wept for a long time.

For many years, I had blamed God for not stopping this horrible act of violence. But He had been there. Understanding this brought this verse to my mind: "But he was wounded for our transgressions, he was bruised for our iniquities: the chastisement of our peace was upon him; and with his stripes we are healed" (Isaiah 53:5 KJV). This truth set me free from the resentment I'd had towards God.

At the beginning of my inner healing journey, my family and I spent a few days at the Elijah House in Spokane. There, I had one of the most profound encounters I've ever had with Jesus. Sitting down next to me, the prayer minister asked the Holy Spirit to guide me to the very first time in my life I wanted to die. I discovered it was when I was in my mom's womb. I could hear the loud voices outside of the womb— a verbal fight that often went on for days or months. I was anxious, and I didn't know if I was the reason for the fight. I didn't want to hear but there was no place to go. I felt stuck and hopeless. That was the first time I wanted to die.

The prayer minister guided me to repent of wanting to die. I forgave those who had fought and shouted, and I forgave myself for accepting the blame for it all. As I was repenting and forgiving, I saw a light coming near. It was Jesus, rowing a boat towards me to come and rescue me. I sobbed uncontrollably for a very long time. He did come to rescue me. His very presence was the Light that invaded the darkness of hopelessness I'd been carrying.

I want to share Nancy's story with you. My husband and I have ministered to her in prayer. Nancy encountered God during inner healing sessions that completely transformed her self-image and self-worth.

Nancy's father had sexually violated her since she was a child and all the way through her teenage years. When she became a Christian, there always remained a distance between her and the heavenly Father. She didn't want to be close to the Father God as she projected the image of her earthly father onto her heavenly Father.

During the prayer session she forgave her father and, most importantly, she forgave herself for not being able to stop her father from hurting her. She had always seen herself as "dirty and unclean," which led her to do "dirty and unclean" things. Guided by the Holy Spirit, I asked if she would be willing to forgive her five-year-old self. She replied she would.

It took a lot of courage to revisit and confront the issue of her father's abuse of her five-year-old self. She saw the little Nancy dressed in filthy dirty rags. She forgave her father. I then invited the little Nancy to accept Jesus as her Savior. As soon as she said yes, the picture in her mind changed: little Nancy immediately became clean and her dirty rags became a white dress as Nancy the child ran to the throne to embrace Jesus as her Savior. She then saw Jesus holding the hands of both the grown-up Nancy and little Nancy as they happily walked together. In the past, she'd hated little Nancy, blaming and rejecting her. After this prayer session, she reconnected with and embraced the child within her. She finally felt whole. She now sees herself as a beautiful bride of Jesus, wearing a pure white dress.

Gideon, who delivered Israel from the Midianites, didn't see himself as God saw him. He saw himself through tainted lenses. "Oh Lord, how shall I deliver Israel? Behold, my family is the least in Manasseh, and I am the youngest in my father's house" (Judges 6:15). Meanwhile, the angel of the Lord had called him a "valiant warrior" (Judges 6:12). The Lord continued to encourage him. "Surely, I will be with you, and you shall defeat Midian as one man" (Judges 6:16).

Gideon's tainted lenses through which he saw himself as small and unworthy started to come off through his engagement and encounters with the Lord. His view of himself became more and more aligned with how God saw him—a mighty man of valor—as he obeyed God's voice. With an army of only three hundred men, Gideon defeated the multitudes of Midianites by blowing trumpets and shouting around the enemy's camp. It was amazing. The enemies fought against themselves and Israel utterly defeated the Midianites, exactly as God had told him.

In the Father's throne room, people encounter the Trinity—Father, Son, and Holy Spirit. There is a divine exchange of lies for truth and healing takes place. The lens of love replaces tainted lenses. During an inner healing session, an encounter in the Father's throne room may go something like this:

"The Holy Spirit guides you to the Father's throne room," I tell John who had come for prayer. "Please tell us what you see, hear, and sense."

"The throne room is two floors big," John says, "and there is a giant throne. The Father is on the throne; Jesus stands on the floor in front of the Father. I stand on the left side of the throne. The Holy Spirit is floating in the air."

"Are you willing to go to the Father and sit on His lap?"

"Hmm, not really."

"Holy Spirit, would you show him what lies he's believing about the Father?"

"I am not worthy of his love," John says.

"Are you willing to renounce the lie that you are not worthy of His love?"

"Yes," John says, and repeats the prayer.

"Where are you now?" I ask.

"I am sitting on the Father's lap."

"Father, who do You say he is to You?"

"I belong to Him. He is pleased with me."

"Thank you, Father."

"I have always felt lonely and was by myself since I was a child."

"Holy Spirit, would You show him when he started to feel this way?"

"It is when I was seven years old," John says, "and I was by myself most of the time. I see myself in a school soccer field."

"Was Jesus there with you on the soccer field?"

"No. Wait, yes; He was behind me."

"I've had a revelation: it was after school; nobody was on the soccer field but somehow I was expecting people to be there."

"How do you feel about this expectation?"

"I felt lonely; I thought nobody liked me and they didn't want to play soccer with me in this empty field."

"Ask God: does this expectation come from Him?"

"No, it isn't from God."

"When your expectation doesn't come from God, it can bring bitterness into your relationship with your schoolmates."

"Oh, I just realized I had the same type of expectations about my boss and other authority figures. That might be the reason for all the pain in those relationships. I repent of all these expectations that are not from God."

"Please pray this with me," I say to John. "Lord, I give all the pain to You and ask for a divine exchange."

John repeats the prayer and a few seconds later says, "He has given me a diamond heart."

"Would you be willing to give your heart in exchange for the diamond heart He has given you?" I ask.

John is silent and after a long pause says, "Some parts of my heart say yes, some parts say no."

"Would you look at your heart and let me know what you see?"

"There is a wound in the bottom left of my heart. It's related to all the difficulties I have gone through during the last few years. I said 'yes' to God, but that yes led to all these difficulties and pain."

"What is the truth from God?"

"It doesn't mean it's not God's will when there are difficulties."

"Are you willing to hand over all your pain to God?"

"Yes."

"What does your heart look like now?"

"The wound is being healed," John says.

John had tainted lenses in viewing God, making Father God unapproachable; Jesus wasn't there for him and God wasn't trustworthy. He viewed himself through tainted lenses as well: he's not worthy of God's love, and he's abandoned and lonely. After this encounter in the throne room, the taints on his lenses were removed and he received a new, healed heart.

Questions to ponder:

+ *When was the last time you encountered Jesus?*
+ *How has the encounter with God changed your tainted lenses?*

PART 4

THROUGH THE LENS
OF LOVE

18

MIRACLES

Surrender and Trust

A miracle is a shift in perception from fear to love.

—*Marianne Williamson*

My grandparents on my father's side lived much of their lives in separate houses after their children were born. My grandfather played Mahjong, which is a kind of gambling game. At one time, he lost so much money, the other player took his wife away. He fell into depression until someone told him to go to church and ask God to help him. Desperate, he didn't have much choice so he decided to give church and Jesus a try. There he accepted Jesus and determined not to gamble ever again.

It must have been supernatural because he never did gamble again, and his children never got into gambling. However, his wife was still in the custody of the other gamblers. He had to pay the debts to get his wife back, but he was penniless. The pastor of the church decided to pay the debts so my grandmother could come back home.

My grandfather became a faithful churchgoer because of such extraordinary kindness. But it didn't convince my grandmother who remained a devoted Buddhist. There was never peace between them due to their different religious beliefs and they ended up living in separate places. My grandmother lived with her daughter, and my grandfather lived alone.

When you see the world through the lens of hatred, peace is nowhere to be found. You always encounter conflict, confrontation, and separation. Each generation has the opportunity to invite God into our lives. Therefore, we have the choice and power to redeem the generational dysfunctions and redirect the family line to receive God's blessings.

My grandfather's faith did not pass on to his children. Among all the grandchildren, I was chosen by God to come to the United States and picked up the torch of faith in Jesus. My grandfather and my father's generations had struggled for survival. I went to the United States in search of a better life. God has supplied abundantly beyond what I could ever imagine and ask.

Due to my dysfunctional family lines on both my mother's and father's sides, I grew up in an unhappy home. Was there hope for me ever to have a good marriage? That was the question in my mind for a very long time. Merriam-Webster defines a miracle as "an extraordinary event manifesting divine intervention in human affairs." My marriage was a miracle by this definition.

In my late thirties, I had a burning desire to have a family of my own and was acutely aware of my ticking biological clock. I had a successful career, despite some bumps along the road. Well-educated and well-traveled, I loved God and served Him faithfully. I'd been told not to pursue God so hotly, as the more I sought God the smaller the pool of available men.

I thought men were intimidated by a professional woman who didn't seem to need a man in her life. Family and friends often set up dates and introductions, but none of these worked out. I even went to a dating agency and tried *E-Harmony.com*; still, I couldn't find my Prince Charming.

I had a list of ten criteria in case Prince Charming did show up; I'd recognize him by crossing off the requirements on my list, one by one. The hope of marrying someone who loves God and who is successful in life grew dimmer and dimmer. And then suddenly, my world was flipped upside down in the career I had pursued so diligently.

After the demotion, I went to an executive coaching session. My coach asked me what would make me happy and content? After I thought about it, I said, "I've had a career. I've always wanted a family of my own; I want to have children as well."

When I look back, the minute I uttered my heart's desire in words, God began to orchestrate circumstances, events, and people to make this happen. It seems God had been waiting for this moment. Upon the confession of my heart's desire, the blessings of a family started to pour into my life.

One Sunday in April 2007, a little time after that coaching session, I attended a different church. After the service, I went up to ask for prayer. The pastor—who knew absolutely nothing about me or my circumstances—said, "God is doing a new thing; He is going to bless you in the area of family."

I had a list; I wanted to decide who would be my future husband. I had a terrible fear that if I let God choose a husband for me, He would make me marry a pastor and then send both of us as missionaries to Africa. This thought terrified me. Deep down in my heart, I didn't trust God to choose the best person for me—He was only interested in making me suffer like Jesus. I was seeing God through my lenses of fear and mistrust.

At the Inner Life Conference in May 2007, I wasn't able to sing the hymn that was so familiar to me: *All to Jesus, I surrender, All to Him, All to Him I freely give. I will ever love and trust Him.* Tears streamed down my face as I was convicted of not fully surrendering to God, especially in the choice of my future husband. On the flight back home, I said sorry to God and told Him I surrendered and I trusted His choice. After I prayed, I lost the fear of being sent away to Africa.

I hadn't been able to discern fear because the lens of fear was so familiar to me. I wanted to control who I would marry, according to my criteria. As soon as I replaced the lens of fear with the lens of trust, the miracle started to unfold.

The blessing overtook me soon after I removed my lens of mistrust and replaced it with the lens of trust. I met my husband two months later, in July. We worked together in an outreach at a detention center for juveniles. We started dating in November and he proposed to me in December. We've been happily married since April 2008.

Miracles do happen. Sometimes, replacing tainted lenses of mistrust and fear with the lens of love opens the way for the miracle to happen.

Questions to ponder:

+ *What are the tainted lenses that are keeping you from experiencing a miracle?*
+ *Have you experienced a miracle when you've replaced tainted lenses with the lens of love?*

19

GENERATIONAL MANDATE

Possessing the Land

*This will be written for the generation to come, that a people
yet to be created may praise the Lord.*

—*Psalm 102:18*

My grandfather was a believer. He was blessed to live
to the age of 83, which was ten years after he'd
been diagnosed with colon cancer, despite having
lived much of his life in poverty and with a lack of nutritious
food. By God's mercy, all his children and grandchildren are
no longer living in poverty. They live in abundance, although
his children didn't believe in God as their father did.

Desperately fleeing from hunger, my grandfather and his
children fixed all their focus and energy on meeting their
physical needs. The lenses with which my grandfather viewed
provision was *it's all up to me*, even after he became a believer.

Manna is the food from heaven and it symbolizes the
fresh revelation of God for everyday living. My grandfather
was given the Word of God as food for his soul and spirit. He

didn't know that man doesn't have to live on bread alone as his focus was to get his stomach fed. "He humbled you and let you be hungry, and fed you with manna which you did not know, nor did your fathers know, that He might make you understand that man does not live by bread alone, but man lives by everything that proceeds out of the mouth of the Lord" (Deuteronomy 8:3).

Because of God's mercy, I—being the third generation—picked up the baton of faith in God. My generation has gone in, fought, and won the battles against some giants in the land. There will be more land for my future generations to go in and possess. God is so gracious and He gives each generation the resources and power to drive out the enemy and possess the land.

Each of our family lines has land through a covenant with God. Each generation is to go in and possess the land which the Lord has given to our forefathers. "All the commandments that I am commanding you today you shall be careful to do, that you may live and multiply, and go in and possess the land which the Lord swore to give to your forefathers" (Deuteronomy 8:1).

If our forefathers had gone in and possessed the land which the Lord swore to give to them, we, as future generations, would live peacefully in the land and enjoy the Lord's blessings. Each generation has a choice to go in and possess the land, which means the enemy in that land has not yet been driven out, and the Lordship of God has not yet been 100% established.

Possessing the land has a lot to do with our hearts. The land is like a heart. Would it be wholeheartedly one with the spirit of God? Our heart is tested on whether or not it fears God and keeps His commandments through a wilderness experience, so that we stay humble and dependent on Him. "You shall remember all the way which the Lord your God has led you in the wilderness these forty years, that He might humble you, testing you, to know what was in your heart, whether you would keep His commandments or not" (Deuteronomy 8:2).

Our heart is not only tested by wilderness experiences but will also be tested by blessings. "Otherwise, when you have eaten and are satisfied, and have built good houses and lived in them, and when your herds and your flocks multiply, and your silver and gold multiply, and all that you have multiplies, then your heart will become proud and you will forget the Lord your God who brought you out from the land of Egypt, out of the house of slavery" (Deuteronomy 8:12–14).

Our God is good, and He wants a good life for His children. "For the Lord your God is bringing you into a good land . . . a land where you will eat food without scarcity, in which you will not lack anything; a land whose stones are iron, and out of whose hills you can dig copper. When you have eaten and are satisfied, you shall bless the Lord your God for the good land which He has given you" (Deuteronomy 8:7, 9–10).

At the end of the day, what will we say? That everything we've done was by our own power, and the wealth we've gained by the strength of our hands? Or, "But you shall remember the Lord your God, for it is He who is giving you power to make wealth, that He may confirm His covenant which He swore to your fathers, as it is this day" (Deuteronomy 8:18).

Our generational mandate is to know and remember that God is good. He is love, faith, and hope in our lives. We will uproot the giants of hatred, injustice, hopelessness, and fear in our family lines.

Questions to ponder:

+ *What is your generational mandate?*
+ *What is the land the Lord has called your generation to possess?*
+ *What are some of the areas where the lordship is not 100% established in the land the Lord has given to your forefathers and your generation?*

20

SIGNIFICANCE IN CHRIST

I Am Who He Says I Am

God is most glorified in me when I am most satisfied in him.
He gets the glory. I get the joy.

—John Piper

I left the world of corporate business more than ten years ago. I could have continued pursuing the path of a successful career woman. Instead, I quit my job and became a stay-at-home mom to care for my children and support my husband's career.

At the start of this new life choice—when I'd finished the day's work, turned on the dishwasher, cleaned the kitchen, taken the trash out, and turned off the light of my household management business for the day—I often wondered if God cared about my heart's desires or not. I was often brought to tears when people prayed for me and talked about *sacrifice*.

One day, after I took my younger daughter to school, I went to a quiet place and had a conversation with God. "God, do you even care about what my heart desires?" To which God replied, "I love you with an everlasting love; your worth is pre-determined; it is in Christ Jesus. Nothing you do can add more worth to yourself. Any addition is a false perception of worth, which is people's opinion of you or your evaluation of your worth. But your value is pre-determined, and it is in Christ Jesus."

I realized I had been striving to be a good Christian, a good daughter to my parents, a good mom, and a good wife. All this striving made me exhausted. I felt sad I might not be able to finish the first draft of my book by mid-June, then mid-August, and then by the end of December 2019. I started to blame all the things that had taken my time: the mission trips, endless housework, driving, helping with the kids' homework, and the ministries of helping others.

All these strivings came from a place of "I need to be in control of all of these." All these doings proved I am worthy. I need to be in control because God is not in control. If I let Him be in control, the outcomes may not be what I desire. After all, my family lines have a long history of suffering injustice and misery. How can I trust God more? How can I surrender more to him?

There was a fierce battle between letting Him or me be the Lord of my life. Eventually, I recognized I was seeing everything through the lens of control (being in charge), which is rooted in fear and not in faith. I repented for taking matters into my own hands. My own hands can only fit two fistfuls of things and I am willing to let everything fall out of my hands and into God's palm. The world is in the palm of His hand.

And so, my conversation with God continued.

"God, please forgive me for controlling my life in the way I wanted. I surrender my life and my ways to you. What is my role when I let go of all of these? How do I partner with you, God? What does it mean my worth is in Christ Jesus?"

"My ways are higher than yours. The wise thing is to ask Me and talk with Me about everything. If I say go, go; if I say no, stop; if I am silent, hold tight and don't move."

"God, is that the partnership you are talking about?"

"It's a good start."

"I'm so sorry. This kind of partnership is very foreign to me. I'm so used to taking control of things and only come to You, God, when it doesn't work out anymore."

"I am pleased with you. You are precious. You are my beloved. You have all the resources from Christ in you to accomplish what I have called you to accomplish. Your dreams are my dreams for you. You are a vessel to achieve my dreams. Partnering with me brings utmost contentment and pleasure, as it brings blessings to so many others and yourself. That is what it means by 'my worth is in Christ Jesus.'"

Hearing God helps me to know my worth. "I am who I AM," says the I Am.

I heard the story of the eight-cow wife from a friend a few years ago and it stuck with me ever since. There are several versions of the story online, many partially based on an article found in the Reader's Digest. The original work was copyrighted by Patricia McGerr in Women's Day, 1965.[1]

The story relates how, on a Pacific island called Kiniwata, the wedding tradition involves a man asking permission from the father of the bride he wants to marry. The suitor must offer a dowry in cows. On this particular island, a decent wife is worth two or three cows; an excellent wife is worth four or five cows. The woman's looks, personality, family, and reputation determine her worth. Women on the island all know each other's values and talk and joke about it. "I'm a three-cow wife," some would say, "and you're only a two-cow wife."

A young man called Johnny Lingo lived on the nearby island of Nurabandi. The brightest and strongest young man in the islands, he was also the richest for he was an excellent trader and knew how to make a deal for anything from fish to pearls. Johnny was known for his keen eye and trading skills. When Johnny came to Kiniwata, he went straight to Sarita's home and asked her father for permission to marry her. Sarita's father thought he would be lucky to trade her for one or two cows for, in his eyes, his daughter was worthless, ugly, and useless. Indeed, in other people's eyes, Sarita was a plain-looking, skinny, shy, and not very happy girl with a hunched back.

The whole island—including Sarita's father—was shocked when Johnny offered eight cows for Sarita's hand in marriage. Some said Johnny must be crazy. The entire island was buzzing about the sharp young trader making the worst deal ever; having traded eight cows for Sarita he'd surely got the short end of the deal. But Johnny fulfilled his promise and delivered eight cows to Sarita's father. That night, after the wedding celebration, he took his bride away to his home on Nurabandi.

Sometime later, an American called Shenkin came to Nurabandi to see Johnny as he wanted to buy some fish and pearls. Johnny welcomed Shenkin into his home. A woman came into the room to place flowers on the table. Shenkin was stunned by her beauty, confidence, and sparkling eyes. Johnny told him she was his wife, Sarita. Shenkin couldn't believe it. She was the most beautiful woman he'd ever seen, and so completely different from the description of her he'd heard back in Kiniwata.

Shenkin couldn't help himself and asked about Sarita's transformation. Johnny explained. "Many things can change a woman. Things happen inside, things happen outside. But the thing that matters most is what she thinks of herself. In Kiniwata, Sarita believed she was worth nothing. Now she knows she is worth more than any other woman in the islands."

Her value came from the esteem in which her husband held her. The beautiful Sarita—who had always existed—emerged as she came to believe and behold her unmatched worth.

Aren't we like Sarita? We don't believe we're worth much. We hide behind the trees regardless of our great Redeemer having come to give Himself for us. We, the believers, are the bride of Christ, purchased by the blood and life of Jesus.

There is no higher price than that in this world, or even in the universe. What matters the most is how we see ourselves: through the lens of a two-cow wife or the lens of an eight-cow wife.

Questions to ponder:

+ *Are you content with who you are as a child of God?*
+ *Do you believe you are significant in Christ?*
+ *Do you—through the lens of love—see, accept, and believe your worth as reflected in the exceptional price paid for you?*

21

INTIMACY WITH GOD

Be Thou My Vision

Royalty is my identity. Servanthood is my assignment.
Intimacy with God is my life source.

—Bill Johnson

According to Wikipedia, "Intimacy involves the feeling of being in a close, personal association, and belonging together. It is a familiar and very close affective connection with another as a result of a bond formed through knowledge and experience of the other. Genuine intimacy in human relationships requires dialogue, transparency, vulnerability, and reciprocity."[1] By this definition, an intimate relationship has three characteristics:

1. A feeling of belonging and close, personal association.

2. A bond through mutual knowledge and experience.

3. A connection where there is dialogue, transparency, vulnerability, and reciprocity.

God is our Creator and He is almighty, holy, and above all. Is it possible for us to have an intimate relationship with God? What would such a close relationship with God look like? I posed the following question to my friends who are more anointed and advanced in their spiritual walk than I: "What does intimacy with God look like in your life?" The answers were varied.

"I start my day praying in the spirit for an hour; I get the download from God while I am communing with Him in the spirit."

"I get a cup of coffee and have a coffee date with God. I talk with Him and He talks with me; there is nothing I wouldn't talk to Him and get His wisdom about. It's like getting together with a good friend."

"God inhabits the praises of His people. I get up at 5:00 am every morning and worship Him; there I meet with Him."

"I walk with God, I commune with Him. He guides my life."

An intimate relationship with God looks different to different people. However, it seems one thing is common to all: a successful and intimate relationship needs some level of discipline.

I found it very challenging to have discipline as a mother of two kids. Even in the mornings, when I can get away and be myself with God before everyone else in the house gets up, I often drift back into sleep and wake up feeling defeated. Now looking back, I could say my lens on intimacy was tainted. I believed a lie that God only shows up during the early morning and there needs to be laborious preparation from my side for Him to show up.

I read about some faith heroes; they spent hours with the Lord. There would be a quantum leap after a period of quantitative effort. I was told not to give up. Wait longer, praise more, repent more, and eventually, He will show up and speak to me. Another tainted lens I have towards intimacy with God is that it is challenging, and it takes a lot of effort to get closer to God.

In 2008, I started to practice waiting on God. I had more time after quitting my corporate job. In the beginning, I would fall asleep but slowly, I began to carry on a conversation with God. One of the teachings that helped me was that of the 17th Century monk, Brother Lawrence, whom *Christianity Today* describes as a "practitioner of God's presence." "In his Maxims, Lawrence writes, 'Men invent means and methods of coming at God's love, they learn rules and set up devices to remind them of that love, and it seems like a world of trouble to bring oneself into the consciousness of God's presence. Yet it might be so simple. Is it not quicker and easier just to do our common business wholly for the love of him?' For Brother Lawrence, 'common business,' no matter how mundane or routine, was the medium of God's love. The issue was not the sacredness or worldly status of the task but the motivation behind it."[2]

I concluded from reading about Brother Lawrence that I could talk to God while doing my chores and managing my household. Most of the time, my mind is on the work at hand. Whenever I become intentional, seeking God to hear what He has to say about a matter, He always responds with wisdom. Still, most of the time, I was seeking counsel from God for only essential issues in life.

During our three years in Hong Kong from 2014 to 2017, my understanding of intimacy with God was seriously challenged. In one of the ministries in which I was involved for a while, the ministry leader believed intimacy with God meant seeking and hearing God in everything—including what clothes and even shoes to wear. This was based on the belief that the color and style of clothes and shoes all had spiritual meanings.

I struggled with this definition of intimacy with God. I searched the Bible and consulted mentors, and I concluded that God *can* speak to us through everything, including nature, events, or animals. There is even evidence of this in the Bible; for example, God spoke to Balaam through a donkey. "And the Lord opened the mouth of the donkey, and she said to Balaam . . ." (Numbers 22:28).

We are so used to relying on our own ways, only seeking and hearing God for the big and seemingly important things. Although I didn't adopt the habit of asking God how to get dressed every morning, I do believe that seeking God in all things—big and small—will bring blessings to our lives. In the wisdom of Solomon, "Trust in the Lord with all your heart and do not lean on your own understanding. In all your ways acknowledge Him, and He will make your paths straight" (Proverbs 3:5-6).

One unforgettable experience I had in seeking God about something seemingly small concerned my smartphone. My younger daughter went to an international Christian school there in Hong Kong. During a school outing, my smartphone fell into the water. I quickly scooped it up out of the water, whereupon it became hot. My husband gave me his old mobile phone to use while we tried to figure out ways of salvaging my baptized smartphone. We sent the damaged phone for repair. A few weeks later, the repaired phone was returned.

While my phone was in the repair shop, something else happened to the phone my husband had loaned me. It was a long walk from the bus station to my daughter's school. Every day, we made our way through a busy open grocery market, up and down elevators, and in amongst residential buildings to get to her school. One day, after dropping off my daughter, I couldn't locate the loaned black smartphone. I panicked and searched everywhere—retracing my steps upstairs and downstairs, up and down the path to school several times—and flipped my handbag again and again, but the loaned smartphone was gone. I filed a police report and didn't hear anything back. How could I lose another phone after dropping one in the water? Anxiety filled my heart and my mind. A new smartphone costs thousands of Hong Kong dollars at that time.

After hours and days of agonizing, I finally decided to ask God about these incidents. What I heard shocked me. "Both phones are registered under your husband's name. You have relied on your husband to hear God's voice." I was immediately convicted. I'm not saying God caused my phones to fall into the water or to get lost but He can use every kind of circumstance—good or bad—to benefit us.

God had probably tried to get my attention for a long time. My antenna was not yet tuned into His frequency. My husband is a godly man who is relatively confident about his ability to hear from God. I naturally seek his advice for every decision: "Honey, what do you think about this?" Further, talking together about everything is one of the foundations for a happy marriage. The problem is that by doing so, I had negated the opportunity of seeking God's counsel directly and thereby belittled my relationship with Him. It was as if God was waving His arms at me. "Hey there! Come and talk with Me, since you want intimacy." Instead of seeking God, my eyes and ears were on man's counsel.

The Bible teaches us differently. "Now set your heart and your soul to seek the Lord your God" (I Chronicles 2:19). Again, "Call to Me and I will answer you, and I will tell you great and mighty things, which you do not know" (Jeremiah 33:3).

In the words of Jesus, "Ask, and it will be given to you; seek, and you will find; knock, and it will be opened to you. For everyone who asks receives, and he who seeks finds, and to him who knocks it will be opened" (Matthew 7:7–8).

God has promised us He will disclose Himself to us on the condition of our having and keeping His commandments. Our love to God is shown by our obedience in our hearts, attitudes, and actions to His commandments. "He who has My commandments and keeps them is the one who loves

Me; and he who loves Me will be loved by My Father, and I will love him and will disclose Myself to him" (John 14:21). Intimacy with God is possible as demonstrated by Jesus. "I and the Father are one" (John 10:30). Oneness with God is the ultimate intimacy.

Questions to ponder:

+ *Are you intimate with God?*
+ *What are the tainted lenses that may hinder your intimacy with God?*

22

JOURNEY TO THE PROMISED LAND

Walk with God

I will give to you and to your descendants after you,
the land of your sojournings, all the land of Canaan,
for an everlasting possession; and I will be their God.

—Genesis 17:8

I found hope when I found God. To me, personally, God is the author of living hope. When I didn't know God, my world and my future were all up to me and my efforts. When I came to know God, the tainted lenses of self-reliance, which were from the fear of abandonment, fell off. Knowing that God is rooting for me, and His goodness and faithfulness are in my everyday life, keeps the hope alive.

Looking back, God with His perfect love has cast out some giants of fear. I no longer live in fear of being abandoned by God, or in fear of failure, or evil forces. Yet, I still need to let the perfect love of God drive out some other fears in my life. My prayer is that God will let me know and experience

His perfect love each and every day, that He will let me grow in the knowledge and understanding of His perfect love that casts out all fear.

Seeing through the lens of love is a process, not a destination. I have not fully restored the lens of love in every aspect of my life. The journey of shedding our tainted lenses continues until we see Jesus face to face. "For now we see in a mirror dimly, but then face to face; now I know in part, but then I will know fully just as I also have been fully known" (1 Corinthians 13:12).

Restoring our 20/20 vision of the lens of love is a process and it requires the work of the Holy Spirit in us. It is essentially by the sanctification of the Holy Spirit that we become wholly identified with Jesus Christ and grow into the full measure of Christ. God is passionate about us being able to see through the lens of love.

We are not on this journey alone. He has sent the Holy Spirit to help us. The Holy Spirit will reveal the taints of our lenses, gently and with grace, if we pay attention to Him. The Holy Spirit also enables us to remove the taints from our lenses when we humble ourselves. "According to the foreknowledge of God the Father, by the sanctifying work of the Spirit, to obey Jesus Christ and be sprinkled with His blood: May grace and peace be yours in the fullest measure" (1 Peter 1:2).

God Himself also guides us with His eye. "I will instruct you and teach you in the way which you should go; I will counsel you with My eye upon you" (Psalm 32:8). We often talk about focusing on God and the need to look Him in the eye for instruction—His teaching of truth and wisdom to walk on the right path. When our lens locks into His lens of love, we are on the path of abundant life.

You will know a tree by its fruit. A good tree bears good fruit. We will know if our lenses are restored to the lens of love by the fruit of the Spirit: "But the fruit of the Spirit is love, joy, peace, patience, kindness, goodness, faithfulness, gentleness, self-control" (Galatians 5:22–23).

These are the fruits of the Spirit, not the fruits of our self-effort. Our job is to stay connected to the vine and allow the Holy Spirit to bear fruit in us. When we are sensitive to the prompting, revealing, and guidance of the Holy Spirit in getting rid of our tainted lenses, we allow the Holy Spirit to bear fruit in us. Replacing our lenses of hatred, fear, hopelessness, injustice, pride, and bitterness with the lens of love allows the Spirit to bear fruit of love, joy, peace, kindness, goodness, faithfulness, gentleness, and self-control in us.

I am more joyful, content, and loving towards God, myself, and others now than I was ten years ago. I didn't have a strategy or method to move from hopelessness to hope, from fear to love, from dissatisfaction to contentment. The Holy Spirit has worked in me and through me to return to the lens of love. The only thing I have done consistently is never letting go of God and His ways.

I recommend you find a quiet place where you won't be interrupted and go through the steps listed below. And let me know how it goes with you.

1. Repent from unrighteousness (i.e. idolatry, pride, hatred, fear, control, self-reliance).

2. Humble yourself; step down from your high horse. Return to the reverence of God; submit to His authority and Lordship, and believe that He is good.

3. Forgive.

4. Remember and meditate on God's goodness in your life.

5. Put on the lens of love and see God for who He is.

6. Put on the lens of love and see who you are in Christ.

7. Put on the lens of Jesus and see others (especially the ones who irritate you the most) as God sees them.

My prayer for you is that after you read my journey and my stories and the stories of others, you will receive healing and find the keys to restoring the lens of love in your life so you will experience greater intimacy with God, find peace in your relationships, and discover contentment in life.

I believe in you. I pray that you will have the courage to examine the tainted lenses in your lives—from cultural settings through generational patterns to significant life events. It brings utmost joy to Father God and me when you replace your tainted lenses with the lens of love. I cannot wait to hear stories of your bravery and the joy of your intimate walk with the Lord Jesus Christ.

ENDNOTES

CHAPTER 2: LACK OF VISION

1. Lee PP1, Spritzer K, Hays RD, *The Impact of Blurred Vision on Functioning and Well-Being*, National Center for Biotechnology Information, Ophthalmology, March 1997, https://www.ncbi.nlm.nih.gov/pubmed/9082261
2. Christopher Ingraham, *Americans are getting more miserable, and there is data to prove it*, Washington Post, March 22, 2019, https://www.washingtonpost.com/business/2019/03/22/americans-are-getting-more-miserable-theres-data-prove-it/
3. Gregory Scott, in an online discussion about "through the lens" as an idiom and not as in photography, October 21, 2016, https://www.quora.com/What-does-it-mean-through-the-lens-mean-as-a-idiom-and-not-as-in-photography

CHAPTER 3: ORIGINAL LENS

1. Attributed to Dallan Forgaill, translated from ancient Irish to English by Mary E. Byrne in Eriú, *Be Thou My Vision*, Journal of the School of Irish Learning, 1905, and versified by Eleanor H. Hull,1912, http://www.hymntime.com/tch/htm/b/e/t/h/bethoumv.htm

Chapter 5: Are You Afraid?

1. Dick Eastman, *Intercessory Worship: Combining Worship and Prayer to Touch the Heart of God*, April 16, 2012, pages 195-198, Google Books Preview, https://www.google.com/books/edition/Intercessory_Worship/DMK2j-ijdHYC?hl=en&gbpv=1&printsec=frontcover

Chapter 6: Do You Feel Dissatisfied?

1. Lupita Nyong'o's Speech on *Black Beauty Essence Black Women #BringBackOurGirls*, YouTube video, 4:55, posted by Jaxsprat's Unique Collectibles on March 1, 2014, https://youtu.be/ZPCkfARH2eE

Chapter 7: Visit the Optometrist

1. Refractive Errors, National Eye Institute, https://www.nei.nih.gov/learn-about-eye-health/eye-conditions-and-diseases/refractive-errors
2. Ibid.
3. Ibid., https://www.nei.nih.gov/sites/default/files/2019-06/Astigmatism.pdf

Chapter 8: Tainted Lenses— A Spiritual Perspective

1. A.W. Tozer, https://www.goodreads.com/quotes/376518-what-comes-into-our-minds-when-we-think-about-god

Chapter 9: Tainted Lenses— A Historical Perspective

1. A.R. Bernard, Twitter, @ARBernard, May 7, 2017, https://twitter.com/arbernard/status/861181398522236928?lang=en

2. Susan Adams, Forbes, *Unhappy Employees Outnumber Happy Ones By Two To One Worldwide*, October 10, 2013, https://www.forbes.com/sites/susanadams/2013/10/10/unhappy-employees-outnumber-happy-ones-by-two-to-one-worldwide/?sh=647f7dc6362a

3. Jim Clifton, *The World's Broken Workplace*, June 13, 2017, https://news.gallup.com/opinion/chairman/212045/world-broken-workplace.aspx

4. Søren Kierkegaard, Danish Christian philosopher and theologian, https://en.wikiquote.org/wiki/S%C3%B8ren_Kierkegaard

5. Rick Warren, *The Purpose Driven Life: What on Earth Am I Here For?*, Zondervan Publishing Company, February 1, 2007

6. Elizabeth Smart, *My Story*, October 7, 2013, https://www.goodreads.com/quotes/7796749-then-while-the-other-members-of-my-family-were-waiting

CHAPTER 10: TAINTED LENSES— A SOUL PERSPECTIVE

1. Yves I-Bing Cheng, M.D., M.A., *The Lamp of The Body is the Eye*, http://www.meetingwithchrist.com/E040%20The%20lamp%20of%20the%20body%20is%20the%20eye%20-%20Mt%206(22-23).htm

2. Thayer's Greek Lexicon, https://biblehub.com/thayers/2917.htm

3. Jessica Jones, *Love What You Have: A Real Truth about Why You Always Complain or How to Get Maximum from Your Life Today*, Kindle, 2016

4. Dean Trune, *The Root of a Complaining Spirit is . . .* , December 22, 2011, http://iimin.org/deantrune/2011/12/the-root-of-a-complaining-spirit-is/

5. John Bevere, *How Complaining Halts Your Destiny*, Charisma Magazine, https://www.charismamag.com/

THE LENS OF LOVE

spirit/spiritual-growth/17508-john-bevere-how-complaining-halts-your-destiny

6. Sherri Langton, *The Danger of Complaining*, CBN, https://www1.cbn.com/danger-complaining

7. Shannon L. Alder, Goodreads, Quotes, https://www.goodreads.com/quotes/682006-often-those-that-criticise-others-reveal-what-he-himself-lacks

8. Socrates, Goodreads, Quotes, https://www.goodreads.com/quotes/472923-strong-minds-discuss-ideas-average-minds-discuss-events-weak-minds

9. Jack Canfield, Mark Victor Hansen and Kimberly Kirberger, *The Gossiper*, from *Chicken Soup for the Teenage Soul*, August 28, 2012, https://www.chickensoup.com/book-story/38756/the-gossiper

10. Marshall Goldsmith, *10 Belief Triggers that Sabotage Your Success,* February 15, 2015, https://www.marshallgoldsmith.com/articles/41-10-belief-triggers-that-sabotage-your-success/

11. U. of Alberta, Sexual Assault Centre, *What is a Trigger?*, https://psychcentral.com/lib/what-is-a-trigger/

12. Mark Twain, Goodreads, Quotes, https://www.goodreads.com/quotes/130577-when-people-do-not-respect-us-we-are-sharply-offended

13. "Bitter," Cambridge Dictionary, https://dictionary.cambridge.org/us/dictionary/english/bitter

14. Shari Roan, *"Bitterness as Mental Illness?"* Los Angeles Times, May 25, 2009, https://www.latimes.com/la-he-bitterness25-2009may25-story.html

15. Sheri Jacobson, *Bitterness—Why It Is a Real Psychological Concern*, Harley Therapy Counselling Blog, May 12, 2015, https://www.harleytherapy.co.uk/counselling/bitterness.htm

16. Elizabeth Cohen, *Blaming others can ruin your health*, CNN, August 18. 2011, http://www.cnn.com/2011/HEALTH/08/17/bitter.resentful.ep/index.html

17. Lynn Hare, *Caroline Leaf: Forgive! Part 2 of 4*, May 14, 2014, https://www.lynnhare.com/caroline-leaf-forgive-part-2-of-4/

CHAPTER 11: REPENTANCE

1. *Hebrew Roots/The original foundation/Repentance*, Wikibooks, https://en.wikibooks.org/wiki/Hebrew_Roots/The_original_foundation/Repentance

CHAPTER 12: FORGIVENESS

1. Trudy Bourgeois, Contributor, *The Greatest Gift— To: You and I, From: Nelson Mandela*, Huffpost, February 18th, 2014, https://www.huffpost.com/entry/the-greatest-gift_b_4469297
2. Lorie Johnson, *The Deadly Consequences of Unforgiveness*, CBN News, June 22, 2015, https://www1.cbn.com/cbnnews/healthscience/2015/june/the-deadly-consequences-of-unforgiveness

CHAPTER 20: SIGNIFICANCE IN CHRIST

1. Patricia McGerr, *Johnny Lingo's Eight-Cow Wife*, Condensed from Woman's Day, November 1965, Reader's Digest pp. 138-141, February 1988 https://orion.math.iastate.edu/hentzel/class.545.10/Johny

CHAPTER 21: INTIMACY WITH GOD

1. Intimate Relationship, Wikipedia, https://en.wikipedia.org/wiki/Intimate_relationship
2. Christianity Today, https://www.christianitytoday.com/history/people/innertravelers/brother-lawrence.html

TAINTED LENSES ASSESSMENT

An intimate relationship requires seeing up close. Our relationship with God, self, and others depends on the clarity of our spiritual lenses. This questionnaire is designed to help you assess the tainted lenses that hinder your relationships.

Please answer the thirty questions with a number between *1* and *10*, *1* being the lowest score, and *10* being the highest.

For example, for the first statement, "I am a victim of my circumstance", your response of *1* would mean you strongly disagree (that is, "I am not a victim"); *5* would mean you are indifferent (that is, "Sometimes or in some areas of my life, I am a victim, while at other times or in other areas of my life, I am not a victim"); *10* would mean you strongly agree ("Yes, I am a victim").

If your total score for the thirty questions is 50 or higher, you may want to deal with your tainted lenses to clarify your vision to see God, yourself, and others with a fresh perspective.

1. I am a victim of my circumstance   _____
2. I feel like an orphan, I have to do everything myself   _____
3. My significance and worth are based on my achievements   _____
4. I have lot of fear (e.g., fear of death, fear of failure, fear of rejection, fear of insignificance, fear of sickness, fear of poverty)   _____

5. I hate God _____

6. I hate people _____

7. I hate and blame myself _____

8. I will seek revenge for the wrongs others have done to me, either with action or with words _____

9. The most important thing in my life is to have financial security (money, house, cars, comfortable or luxury lifestyle, etc.) _____

10. The most important thing in my life is to have social status (prestige, property, power, influence, or fame) _____

11. The most important thing in my life is to be recognized for what I do and my accomplishments _____

12. The most important things in my life are my family and friends _____

13. I am easily irritated by others, especially those who hold different points of view from me _____

14. I am often irritated towards those whom do not meet my expectation _____

15. In my mind, I rehearse past failures _____

16. I have opinions about everyone and everything; I like to give my opinion on many things _____

17. I care about what other people think of me _____

18. I like to complain when things do not go my way _____

19. It is easy for me to see and point out mistakes, inadequacies, and problems in others _____

20. I like to talk about people and their problems behind their back   _____

21. I have strong reactions when I perceive negative attitudes, actions, or words towards me   _____

22. I am easily offended by someone's actions or words   _____

23. It is difficult for me to forgive others and forget what they have done to me   _____

24. I do not have a relationship with God   _____

25. I am dissatisfied with my life   _____

26. I rarely hear God's affirmation for me, that I am loved, and I belong to Him   _____

27. God is not a good father, protector, or provider to me   _____

28. I strive to gain approval from others   _____

29. I strive to prove to people that I can do it   _____

30. I don't accept or agree with whom God says I am   _____

Total Score   _____

ABOUT THE AUTHOR

Wei Wei Chang is the founder of Imagine Life Coaching LLC. Through her writing, coaching, and speaking, she helps individuals find fulfillment through an intimate relationship with God.

For many years, Wei Wei struggled to find her voice and purpose. She emigrated from China to the United States as a young student, where she gained a Ph.D. in Economics. After a successful corporate career at a Fortune 500 company, Chang chose to follow a new and different path towards a deeper relationship with God. Over the past ten years, she has helped many people to experience freedom through inner healing.

Wei Wei lives in Arizona with her husband, Steve, and two daughters.

Connect at www.weiweichang.com

Made in USA - Kendallville, IN
1200738_9781647465391
11.28.2020 0845